MW00720534

Comments on other *Amazing Stories* from readers & reviewers

"Tightly written volumes filled with lots of wit and humour about famous and infamous Canadians."
Eric Shackleton, *The Globe and Mail*

"The heightened sense of drama and intrigue, combined with a good dose of human interest is what sets Amazing Stories *apart."*
Pamela Klaffke, *Calgary Herald*

"This is popular history as it should be... For this price, buy two and give one to a friend."
Terry Cook, a reader from Ottawa, on **Rebel Women**

"Glasner creates the moment of the explosion itself in graphic detail...she builds detail upon gruesome detail to create a convincingly authentic picture."
Peggy McKinnon, *The Sunday Herald*, on **The Halifax Explosion**

"It was wonderful...I found I could not put it down. I was sorry when it was completed."
Dorothy F. from Manitoba on **Marie-Anne Lagimodière**

"Stories are rich in description, and bristle with a clever, stylish realness."
Mark Weber, *Central Alberta Advisor*, on **Ghost Town Stories II**

"A compelling read. Bertin...has selected only the most intriguing tales, which she narrates with a wealth of detail."
Joyce Glasner, *New Brunswick Reader*, on **Strange Events**

"The resulting book is one readers will want to share with all the women in their lives."
Lynn Martel, *Rocky Mountain Outlook*, on **Women Explorers**

E.P.L. - JPL

KAREN KAIN

AMAZING STORIES®

KAREN KAIN

Canada's Prima Ballerina

BIOGRAPHY

by Melanie Jones

PUBLISHED BY ALTITUDE PUBLISHING CANADA LTD.
1500 Railway Avenue, Canmore, Alberta T1W 1P6
www.altitudepublishing.com
1-800-957-6888

Copyright 2005 © Melanie Jones
All rights reserved
First published 2005

Extreme care has been taken to ensure that all information presented in
this book is accurate and up to date. Neither the author nor the
publisher can be held responsible for any errors.

Publisher	Stephen Hutchings
Associate Publisher	Kara Turner
Editor	Jennifer Nault
Digital Photo Colouring	Bryan Pezzi

We acknowledge the financial support of the Government
of Canada through the Book Publishing Industry Development
Program (BPIDP) for our publishing activities.

Altitude GreenTree Program
Altitude Publishing will plant twice as many trees as were used
in the manufacturing of this product.

National Library of Canada Cataloguing in Publication Data

Jones, Melanie
    Karen Kain / Melanie Jones.

(Amazing stories)
ISBN 1-55439-017-6

    1. Kain, Karen, 1951- 2. Ballerinas--Canada--Biography.
I. Title. II. Series: Amazing stories (Calgary, Alta.)

GV1785.K28J64 2005   792.8'092   C2005-903553-6

Amazing Stories® is a registered trademark of Altitude Publishing Canada Ltd.

Printed and bound in Canada by Friesens
2 4 6 8 9 7 5 3 1

To Karen and all the other women in my life who worked hard through the best and the worst.

Karen Kain (2002)

Contents

Prologue

Karen almost collapsed as she came flying past the backstage curtains. She gasped for breath. As a ballerina, all her movements had to seem effortless, as though she floated on air. In reality, she had just performed the equivalent to a 400-metre sprint. Her heart was pounding, and she struggled to catch her breath. As she waited backstage, she heard the dramatic music fill the theatre. The stage lights were almost blinding, but through the glare she could see Denys Gagnon dancing Don José's powerful solo. Tonight she was Carmen, and in a few moments, she would return to the stage concealing a knife. But first, she had to tend to the agony in her foot.

Karen had injured her right foot a few weeks earlier, landing poorly from a jump. All the muscles and tendons were either torn or inflamed, but there was no time to rest. She quickly limped over to the stagehand, who had her ice pack waiting. She didn't have much time, but she shoved the ice directly against her skin, hoping to freeze her foot enough to finish the act. Counting the beat of the music, she figured she had 20 seconds left. She frantically tied up her pointe shoe as she heard the music change. Pushing other dancers out of the way, she ran to make her entrance, diving through layers of heavy velvet curtain to reach the stage. Carmen burst into the spotlight, a spurned seductress dressed in red. She flew toward Don José clutching the knife behind her back ...

Chapter 1
The First Giselle

Karen wore her prettiest pink dress, which was bolstered with layers of crinoline. Her black patent leather shoes squeaked as she twisted her hips back and forth, watching the circle of her skirt flare out around her. Winifred, her mother, bent down and gave her a ticket. "Be careful with this," she said. Karen, suddenly serious, held onto it with both hands. It was Karen's eighth birthday, and her parents had driven to Hamilton so she could see the National Ballet of Canada perform *Giselle*. A thrill of excitement bubbled up and Karen raised her arms and spun around. She skipped a few steps before she slowed her pace and began walking sombrely toward the theatre's entrance. Karen's parents watched her enter, glanced meaningfully at each other, and followed her into the theatre.

The house lights filled the theatre with a dim warmth. The velvet seats were red and the ceiling impossibly tall. Karen scooted into her seat, almost unable to contain herself. Still too short to see over an adult's head, she sat on a coat, which her mother had folded and tucked beneath her. The lights dimmed, and in the dark, Karen's small hand flew into her mother's. The music began — a slow and haunting melody in a minor key.

When the stage lights came on, a new world appeared — a small village where the townspeople were dancing to celebrate the harvest. A young peasant woman was separated from the festivities, dancing on her own. When she moved, it was as though she floated on air. A young man named Loys joined her onstage. He was clearly taken by her beauty. Loys pursued her, but she resisted. He came toward her again, softer this time, with a pledge of love and marriage. She accepted, and then they danced together as if no one else existed. Off to the side of the stage, another man looked on with contempt and jealousy. He loved Giselle and wanted her for his own. In the darkness of the audience, a little girl's eyes shone like spotlights.

A hunting party arrived onstage with loud horns and fanfare. Everyone in the village bowed low as the men dismounted to join the festivities. The party was looking for a local nobleman by the name of Count Albrecht. His father and his fiancée, Bathilde, were with them. As the men talked with the villagers, Princess Bathilde met Giselle. The two women discussed their engagements with excitement. Meanwhile, Hilarion, the man who loved Giselle, examined the family crest on the horses and carriage. He picked up Loys's sword and cape, finding the very same crest. Loys was not who he appeared to be! Seizing his chance to set things right, Hilarion burst into the throng of villagers, brandishing Count Albrecht's belongings.

Late in Act I, while other children fussed and dragged their harried mothers to the bathroom, Karen sat spellbound. Giselle was going mad with grief. Her lover had spurned her, and was marrying another. She moved in anguish, her hair loose and flying. The villagers looked on in confusion. Albrecht was tortured; he wanted to go to her, but he couldn't. He had been promised to another. His fiancée looked at Giselle with pity. Distressed, Giselle snatched up Albrecht's sword, and brought it to her chest, collapsing in a heap.

The woman onstage dancing Giselle was Celia Franca — a compact dancer with dark hair and striking features. She was also the artistic director of the ballet. That evening, eight-year-old Karen could not have known how important Celia Franca would become in her life. On the way home, Karen was quiet, gazing out the window of her parents' car as the Hamilton streetlights blurred by. Karen didn't see them. All she saw was a young woman onstage, dancing alone to the music.

The next day, Karen could speak of little else. On her way to school, she skipped and gestured, bending grandly to pluck a dandelion from a neighbour's lawn. When she finally arrived at school, it was dead silent. The playground was empty and the doors closed. She was late. Panicked, Karen pulled open the heavy orange door and slipped inside. That afternoon, her teacher asked them to describe themselves in words and pictures. Karen drew a picture of herself dressed as Giselle in peasant clothing — dancing.

Karen had been attending ballet classes for a couple of years by that time, but she started to take them more seriously. In Mrs. Carey Love's studio in Hamilton, Karen would lose herself in the *adagio*, almost in a trance as she danced the combination. In her mind, she was Giselle after her death, a young peasant girl transformed into a dancing spirit. Her movements were light, filled with the sorrow and sadness of a woman betrayed. After class, parents commented that Karen seemed overtaken by the music. This was the beginning of not only a lifelong love of dance, but also a career supported by Karen's musicality and ability to lose herself in a role.

One evening, Karen's teacher waited until most of the parents had gathered up their children and belongings and gone home. Betty Love was a kind woman in her mid-forties, who ran the rudimentary classes out of a small storefront studio. She had taken ballet when she was a girl. Betty had seen real talent in Karen, but knew that she wasn't experienced enough to take Karen as far as she could go. None of her students had ever shown this much promise. Betty made her way over to Karen and Winifred, bending down to pick up Karen's duffle bag. She stood holding the bag and smiled at Karen, who was taking off her ballet slippers. "You know, Mrs. Kain, Karen really has something special," Betty began. Wynn nodded absently before looking up at her, "Oh, thank you, Mrs. Love. She really does enjoy herself." Betty handed Karen's things to Wynn, stood up a little taller, and offered, "I think she should audition for the National Ballet School in Toronto." Wynn stood frozen, taken by surprise. Karen looked up at Betty. She was thrilled.

On the way home, Karen flipped through the brochures Betty had given them. She chattered away about what it would be like to become a real ballerina, asking Wynn question after question about Toronto life. Wynn was quiet on the drive home. She had much bigger things on her mind.

At only 10 years of age, Karen was too young to live away from home, Wynn felt. Dance was a hobby, certainly not a respectable career. Women who danced professionally had loose morals, she believed. And what about Karen's academics? Wynn refused to have her daughter grow up without a proper education. What would she do after her ballet career ended? Everyone knew that ballet dancers were finished by their late twenties. How would Karen make a living? Moreover, the National Ballet School was too expensive — how would they pay?

By the time they arrived home from dance class, Winifred was distraught, but Karen was ecstatic. Charles looked over the brochures with interest. He tried to calm Winifred, but it was pointless. Karen wanted to go to ballet school, and there was nothing her parents could say that would change her mind. It was Charles who agreed to let Karen audition. Besides, he consoled, who says she'll get accepted?

Chapter 2
A Shy Princess

Karen was nervous when she arrived at the National Ballet School with her parents. It was the morning of her audition. She was to join the Grade 11 students for their morning class, and then have a solo audition with Betty Oliphant, the school's principal. Karen was painfully shy, and now she was terrified, surrounded by people she didn't know in a strange studio, miles away from home. Karen had packed and repacked her bag a dozen times the night before, and Wynn helped her get dressed in her tights and leotard. As Karen put on her slippers, Wynn brushed her long, thick hair and wound it into a low bun at the base of her neck. She secured it with hairpins and bent down to kiss her daughter's head. This would be a difficult day for Winifred. She was terribly nervous for her daughter, wanting her to do well, but at the same time wanting to get back into the car and pretend that none of this had ever happened.

Karen entered the studio to join girls who were at least five years older than her. Betty Oliphant stood tall and regal beside the door as the children filed in. Dressed in a tweed skirt and prim blouse, she had a commanding presence. Betty told Karen's parents that the class would take about an hour, and as the door to the studio swung shut, Winifred took a deep breath.

The windowed downtown studio was bright and spacious. Ballet barres lined the walls and several portable barres were moved to the centre of the room. Karen took her place at one of them and stood with her knees pressed together, looking down. Betty swept in and abruptly began leading the girls through a series of bending movements called *pliés* and leg extensions called *tendus*. The exercises were much like Mrs. Love's classes back home in Hamilton, except now Karen's dream of becoming a ballerina was on the line. She concentrated very hard on the movements and danced her best. One girl in the class sobbed loudly and Karen looked back at her with concern. No one said anything to this girl, not her fellow students, nor Betty. They all just kept going as she cried in the corner.

Betty invited the Kains into the studio to watch Karen's solo audition. Winifred and Charles sat nervously to the side, their coats piled onto their laps. Winifred's knuckles stretched white on the strap of her handbag. "Now, young lady," Betty said. "I would like you to leave the studio for a moment, and when you come back, imagine that you are a beautiful princess." Karen's eyes were wide with fear as she walked out of the room. She stared at the floor and her shoulders drooped. The Kains looked at each other as the door closed. Betty glanced over at the couple and smiled. Moments later, the large, dark door creaked open. When Karen entered, she was completely transformed. She walked gracefully to the centre of the room, her back straight and her head held high. At the centre, she turned and looked directly at her subjects — a stricken-looking mother and a grinning father. Then, she scanned the room until her gaze reached Betty. She tilted her head, cast her eyes downward, and gave a low curtsy. Mrs. Kain gasped and burst into tears. Karen stood up, casting a look of uncertainty toward Betty and her mother. Betty suppressed a smile and nodded benevolently. She was impressed.

The next day, Mrs. Kain was in shock as she sat with her husband in Betty's office discussing tuition, school uniforms, and living arrangements. Karen would stay at the school residence, eating, sleeping, and dancing with other would-be ballerinas for the next seven years of her life. Winifred had nothing to worry about in terms of Karen's education. Betty had taken great pains to ensure that every student of the National Ballet School would leave her fold well-prepared for life on "the outside." The Kains were nervous about the cost. Uniforms had to be purchased at Holt Renfrew, a very expensive department store. Tuition was steep — $1700 per year. On an engineer's salary in 1962, and with three other children to support, it would be nearly impossible. Charles and Winifred were both very nervous. Neither of them had ever expected their daughter to be chosen for such a potentially wonderful, yet life-altering opportunity. Could they handle it? Charles took a deep breath, looked at Betty, and nodded firmly.

* * *

While the story of Karen Kain is an inspiring one, the story of the National Ballet of Canada is also incredible. The National Ballet of Canada was created through the efforts of several women at a time when the opinions of women were barely heard. The company's rise to success was against all odds. The world of Canadian ballet began with the pioneering spirit of several disparate women separated by miles of Canadian landscape. By the time the National Ballet of Canada was formed in the early 1950s, the young country was already supporting two fledgling companies in Winnipeg and Montreal. Three wealthy Toronto women, Mrs. Aileen Woods, Mrs. Sydney Mulqueen, and Mrs. Pearl Whitehead, had seen European ballet companies and wanted to elevate Toronto's cultural scene. The women went straight to the top of the ballet world. They flew to London and spoke to Dame Ninette de Valois, the founder and matriarch of the Sadler's

Wells Company in London, one of the most revered ballet companies in the Western world.

Ninette de Valois suggested they find an experienced ballet person from outside Canada to establish and run the company. This was typical of a European mind-set, which assumed that anything European, or specifically British, was best. At the time, it was the only way: no one in Canada knew anything about running a ballet company. Dame Ninette suggested that the ladies try to get Celia Franca, a fine dramatic dancer with the Sadler's Wells Company.

There was, of course, no money for Celia Franca when the three women asked her to make the journey to Canada and conduct a feasibility study in 1951. The T. Eaton Company, the Canadian retail giant, funded Franca's trip to Canada, and gave her a filing job on the top floor of their College Street store in Toronto. When Celia arrived, there were barely any theatres in Canada, and certainly nothing resembling a theatre circuit of any kind. The first years of the company would be fraught with frustration and hilarity as dancers performed in school gymnasiums and town halls as part of the national tours. A temporary board of directors was formed, which consisted of a group of highly influential (and nervous) men and women — they enjoyed the idea of a ballet company, but did not want the financial burden of such a risky venture to fall on their shoulders.

Celia had the idea to run a summer school as a way to assess young talent and generate interest — and hopefully money — for the new company. The board decided that any loss would be from Celia's own pocket. On the condition that she pay them back, they lent her $400 to send out notices and rent the rather run-down St. Lawrence Hall. The huge success of the school convinced the board of the interest in a real ballet company. That August, they agreed to found the National Ballet of Canada. Celia flew off on a national audition tour, and rehearsals began in September 1951.

Beginning as a rather hodgepodge collection of amateur dancers and highly trained administrative staff (Betty and Celia), the company continued to grow with the help of rich patrons and the Canada Council for the Arts. In the company's infancy, Celia Franca danced most of the principal female roles herself. A few of the dancers had training from Europe, but the Canadian population simply didn't have experienced ballet dancers at that time. Celia frequently worked without pay, mounting full-length ballets and organizing tours. These tours would be put off until the last possible moment because of the board's hesitancy to send any money.

In 1958, the National Ballet School was born. Its creation was, once again, a struggle with the board, but a critical victory that may have ensured the company's eventual success. With the addition of the school, Franca could ensure that the next generation of dancers would be properly trained and give the company the credibility she felt it deserved. What she couldn't have known at the time was that the principal of the school, Betty Oliphant, would go on to become one of the world's leaders in ballet training.

Betty Oliphant was a British-born single mother of two. She trained in ballet in England and opened her own dance studio in London at the age of 18 when she realized she was too tall to dance professionally. She married a Canadian man and immigrated in 1947. Soon after, he left her to raise their two children on her own. Betty made ends meet by teaching ballet and tap dance in a studio on Sherbourne Street in Toronto. Later, when the National Ballet Company formed, she acted as rehearsal mistress for their second season, juggling rehearsals and classes in her own studio. Betty was the founding principal of the National Ballet School, the first residential dance-training facility in the country. Her program was very strict, focusing on textbook-perfect technique and top-notch academics. Later in her career, she would be asked to consult for some of the world's most celebrated dance schools, including England's revered Royal Ballet School.

The Canada Council for the Arts was formed in 1957 to support and develop creative endeavours from theatre to visual art to dance. The National Ballet Company had relied on the Canada Council for support since its inception, and in 1960, the company hoped for an even larger grant to undertake some international tours. Instead, the council spent its money on foreign experts, brought over to assess the company in order to determine whether it was worth funding at all. Their report was scathing, but fortunately never distributed.

The ballet's general manager was invited to read it, as long as he didn't show it to Celia Franca — the prevailing rumour was that the company stood to receive $100,000 provided they hire a different artistic director! Celia, of course, stayed with the company, directing its growth for more than 20 years.

In order to bolster the company's national presence, Celia invited Melissa Hayden to dance as the company's first guest artist. The Canadian-born Hayden was dancing with the famous New York City Ballet under George Balanchine. She accepted the offer at once. However, the experience was not as rewarding as Franca had hoped. Hayden made several last-minute changes to the Balanchine dances on the program. She refused to dance with Earl Kraul, the partner chosen for her. She would only allow David Adams to partner her. It was a terrible experience for Adams, as she would panic during the classical pieces and forget the choreography (the New York Company only did contemporary work). Adding insult to injury, Hayden blamed Adams for the mistakes. The critics were thrilled with Hayden's performances and horrified at the apparent ineptitude of the other dancers. Celia simply couldn't win. Respite came later in the 1960s when Erik Bruhn brought his production of *La Sylphide* to the National Ballet of Canada. Bruhn's long-time friend Rudolf Nureyev came to support him, amid cameras and paparazzi. Nureyev ended up performing with the company during one of the evenings, creating quite a stir.

The National Ballet of Canada added several talented

and charismatic principals to their ranks, and gradually it gained some national appreciation. However, it wasn't until 1973, and Karen's explosion onto the international ballet scene, that things really began to take off. But, on a Monday morning in 1962, Karen's story was only just beginning.

Chapter 3
Act I

At exactly 7:00 in the morning on her first day at the National Ballet School, a wake-up bell jarred Karen out of her sleep. Twenty girls flipped back their blankets and got up, rubbing their eyes and making a beeline for the bathrooms down the hall. Karen got up slowly, not knowing what to do. She self-consciously made her bed, trying to make it look like the others. She waited until some of the girls returned from the bathroom before pulling on her regulation pink tights and black leotard. She watched out of the corner of her eye as a group of girls pulled on their school uniforms over top. One of the girls who looked a bit older caught her eye and turned back toward the group. She leaned in, whispered something, and the group giggled. Karen's face burning, she rummaged in her large duffle bag for her warm-up sweats. She grabbed them and slunk off to the bathroom.

The bank of mirrors was packed by the time she got there. Shrill voices and laughter echoed off the walls and the lights seemed too bright. Karen started to panic. She ducked into a cubicle and tried to calm down. By the time she emerged, most of the girls had left. The stragglers finished arranging their hair into tight chignons, glancing at Karen before filing out of the bathroom to the cafeteria for breakfast. Karen gingerly took her place at the mirror. She brushed her long, dark hair, and then something dawned on her. She had never done her own hair. Her mother put her hair into a bun every day before dance class, and Karen didn't know how. Blinking back the tears, she gathered her hair into a low ponytail and ineptly wrapped the elastic band around it. She then crammed her ponytail into one fist and reached for another elastic.

When the bathroom door opened a short time later, Karen was sitting on the ground in tears. Her hair was a rat's nest of elastic bands, wayward bobby pins, lumps, and bumps. A girl about her age stood at the entrance to the bathroom, looking at her. "I'm supposed to find you. You're late for breakfast." Karen sniffed and looked up to see a pretty blonde girl with perfectly controlled hair. The girl smiled and said, "Here. Let me help."

The dancers woke at 7:00 a.m. every day, washed and dressed, and stampeded down to breakfast by 8:00 a.m.

Morning ballet class began at 9:00. After dance class, a full day of academic class ensued, followed by another dance class. The students then ate supper, finished their homework, and were in bed by 9:00 p.m. They wore uniforms to their academic classes and regulation black leotards and pink tights to ballet class. They literally spent every waking (and sleeping) moment with each other.

When Karen took her place at the barre every morning, a very distinct look came into her eyes. It was a look of focus and clarity — as though this was exactly where she was supposed to be. Betty led her students through a structured series of exercises, first at the barre, practising *tendus* and *pliés*. Betty taught her students the Ceccheti method, which was one of the most challenging ballet techniques in the world.

After the barre section of class was over, the dancers took their places at the centre of the room. There, they danced more complicated combinations, learning balance and building strength. One morning, when the accompanist began the music for the *adagio*, Karen was near the back of the class. Neat rows of dancers stretched across the room, all moving in unison, bending and unfolding to the serene composition. The dancers *pliéd*, bending their right knees deeply while dropping their gazes to the floor. Then, bodies slowly expanding as the music swelled, 20 pairs of arms extended and 20 legs lifted high into the air. The music stopped abruptly. "Karen," Betty called from the front, angling her head to catch Karen's eye. "Come to the front, please." Head down, Karen scurried to the front of the class, standing with her heels together and feet slightly turned out in first position. "Now, watch how she fills the phrase, dancers," Betty called out to the class. She nodded at the accompanist and stood back.

As Karen began the combination, she faltered a little, losing her balance. She heard a soft snort of laughter behind her. "Ladies," Betty warned. Karen took a deep breath to compose herself, feeling the stares of her classmates at her back. She listened to the music, its rhythm, and the pull of the crescendos. As the music climbed the scale of notes, Karen's spine grew taller. She followed the music, filling the movements with song and breath. She forgot about Betty and about the girls behind her. She simply danced. When the composition was finished, Karen stood by meekly as Betty scolded the other dancers for their lack of musicality and their stiff way of going through the motions.

After class, some of the girls brushed past Karen, muttering under their breath, and glaring back at her. She was devastated. She had worked so hard to get to the National Ballet School, and now that she was there, it was awful. She loved the dancing, but missed her family and was having trouble making friends. She'd had no idea how competitive the world of ballet could be, and as a sensitive girl, Karen took it all very personally. She ran from the studio to the dormitory in tears. She dialled the familiar phone number, and when her mother answered, Karen began sobbing.

"Karen, darling, what's the matter?" Winifred asked, anxiously.

"They hate me," she cried. Other students stared as they passed her in the hallway. Karen told her mother how much she missed her family. How lonely she felt. How hard everything was. "I hate it here," Karen cried. "I want to come home."

Her mother cooed reassurance into the receiver, but she desperately wanted Karen to come home. Toronto seemed so far away, and the Kains struggled to keep up with the tuition payments. "Pack your bags," Winifred said. "Forget the whole thing."

Gradually, Karen's tears abated, and she felt better. "Well, it's not that bad," she said sniffling. "Maybe I'll give it another week." Karen hung up the phone feeling better, but Winifred was not convinced. She had grave misgivings about the whole arrangement, and she felt like she was being replaced.

Chapter 4
She's Too Fat

The crowd of dancers moved down the hall toward the studios. Confused, Karen followed along, searching the group for someone she knew. She caught the eye of a cute blond boy, who grinned before getting swallowed by the shapeless mass, which eventually formed itself into a line. Karen tapped the shoulder of the girl in front of her. "Why are we lining up?" Karen asked.

"They weigh us every week," the girl replied.

Karen stepped onto the scale a short time later. One of her teachers stood to the side with a clipboard, while another moved the weights along the scale. Betty stood beside the teacher with the clipboard, scanning through the pages now and again. As the teacher at the scale slid the weights farther and farther along, her eyebrows rose in concern. She looked at Karen, scanning her body from head to toe. "You're too fat," she blurted out, shaking her head. She looked rather helplessly at Betty, who came over and looked at the scale.

"Karen, you have to lose weight," she said matter-of-factly. "You'll never have a career in dance."

Stricken, Karen stepped off the scale and walked back to her room. At the age of 12, Karen had reached her full height of five feet and seven inches — tall for a ballerina. She never weighed more than 130 pounds.

Near the end of her first year, Betty invited all of the parents to the school for a demonstration. Charles and Winifred drove in for the day, and sat near the front, looking very proud. The students danced a sequence they had been working on for the past several weeks. Karen danced her heart out, smiling at her parents at every opportunity. During a break, Karen noticed Betty chatting quietly with her parents. Thrilled, she waited until Betty had moved on before rushing up and asking, "What did she say? What did she say?"

Winifred looked at her daughter sympathetically and replied, "She says you're too fat."

This was neither the first nor the last time the Kains would hear this. "She's talented, but she's too fat," would become the mantra of Karen's pre-professional life. Although she was at a medically healthy weight for her height, the ballet aesthetic demanded perfect lines and the appearance of weightlessness. Karen was a healthy, athletic young woman.

There was also the problem of her height. She was bordering on being too tall for the corps, which preferred a uniform height of five feet and six inches, or shorter. Celia Franca had recently had to travel all the way to Europe to search for a male dancer tall enough to partner Martine Van Hamel, who was taller than Karen.

In April of Karen's last school year, Betty pulled her aside one day after class. "Celia Franca has scheduled auditions for the company. You have two weeks to lose weight."

This was everything Karen had been waiting for. She had been studying and working hard at the National Ballet School for seven years, and this was her chance. She loved to dance; it was what she was born to do. She was dancing Odette's solo from *Swan Lake* in the graduation performance; it was one of the most coveted roles in classical ballet, and one of the most difficult. Something was driving Karen, something deep inside her — a combination of ambition and true love. She wouldn't let anything get in her way.

Eating disorders and anorexia in ballet are devastatingly common. George Balanchine, choreographer and artistic director of the New York City Ballet, is often implicated in this severe aesthetic. His contemporary ballet required stick-thin dancers to achieve the perfect look. This has led to an industry-wide standard that is next to impossible to achieve. Ballet dancers turn to extreme measures, eating barely enough to survive, or worse. Gelsey Kirkland, a dancer with the New York City Ballet adopted myriad negative behaviours in order to be a successful ballerina. She starved herself and became anorexic. She turned to drugs, which led to a cocaine addiction. Striving for the illusive ideal of perfection, she underwent several plastic surgeries.

. Lettuce is one of the most popular foods among anorexics because more calories are burned consuming it than it actually contains. This is just one of many tricks used by ballerinas to lose weight. Many dancers wear layers and layers of clothing in class with the intention of sweating the weight off. Some consume little more than coffee or caffeinated diet sodas to give them an energy boost. For two weeks, Karen ate nothing but lettuce and tomatoes, all the while attending class and extra rehearsals for the graduation performance.

With only a few days left to go, Karen was fatigued. She arrived at class, her face looking pale with weariness. There were bags under her eyes and her hair felt like straw to the touch. She took her place at the barre and looked at herself in the mirror. Only five more days, she thought. But after that, would it ever be over? She could barely concentrate on Betty's instructions as the class followed; her voice seemed to be coming through a fog. With every movement, Karen's legs burned as though she had been dancing for hours. She looked at the clock; class had only started 20 minutes ago. Betty led the class through an exercise in second position, a very wide stance. She counted through a large arc with both torso and arms, curving down low and then arching her back up high. Karen already felt light-headed. The large movements were too much, and as she curved her spine all the blood rushed to her head. She stumbled, falling out of her place in line.

Betty came over to her, a look of concern etched into her face. But her eyes were hard. "Are you alright?" she asked. Karen looked at her. She knew there was no other way, no matter how difficult this was. She had to lose the weight or she would never be a ballerina. She nodded. Betty's face softened with relief. "That's my girl," she said, squeezing Karen's shoulder . "Now, go get some water." Karen walked slowly out of the studio, feeling 20 pairs of eyes on her back. Everyone in the class knew what was happening, and no one said a thing. Karen headed straight for the cafeteria and ordered a coffee. She drank it black.

The morning of the audition, Karen woke up almost an hour early. She had barely slept, and peering into the bathroom mirror, she looked it. She was pale and drawn, but she didn't care. After showering and dressing, she coiled her hair with extra attention. The audition would be similar to the class she had been attending for the past seven years. The only difference would be the watchful presence of a regal-looking woman with upswept black hair. Celia Franca stood at the front of the class. She was wrapped in a shawl, her chin turned upward. Her eyes darted from dancer to dancer, assessing body and technique in a matter of seconds. Karen moved with focus and strength, but never seemed to catch Celia's eye. Perhaps Betty was wrong; maybe she didn't have enough talent. By the end of the class, Karen was certain she hadn't distinguished herself at all. It would all come down to the graduation performance.

The next night, when Karen arrived at the theatre, she noticed Betty and Celia standing backstage, watching the dancers warm up. Karen walked onstage and Betty leaned over to whisper something to Celia. Celia looked over at Karen, rolled her eyes skyward, and hissed, "Not another tall one!" Karen closed her eyes and took a deep breath. She was determined not to let anything get in the way of her performance.

Waiting backstage, Karen felt the jangle of her nerves grow silent as the sweet, soulful music began. She was no longer Karen Kain; she was Odette, the beautiful and tragic swan-maiden betrayed by her lover, Prince Siegfried. This particular solo was especially difficult because of the balance and control it required. The role of Odette is challenging for seasoned professionals let alone a young and inexperienced dancer.

For Karen, performing was like freedom. Onstage she could be anyone and do anything, a far cry from the shy girl she was off stage. She came into the first *arabesque* with great concentration; she had to get this right. She lunged forward to prepare, hearing the audience take a collective breath. This was one of ballet's most famous dances, and they knew what was coming. Karen sprung up onto her right pointe shoe. She extended her left leg behind her and lifted it high in the air. She tipped forward, reaching gracefully toward the floor.

She rose up, still balancing on her right leg and spun slowly, beautifully. She floated across the stage, bathed in light.

Karen saw her mother and father in their seats, beaming with pride. She saw her friends from class in the wings, nodding along with the rhythm. She saw Betty smiling proudly, with Celia Franca by her side, gripping Betty's hand. Time seemed to slow down, and Karen felt lifted by the stage lights, as though she was made of air. Karen was exactly where she wanted to be.

On May 23, 1969, Karen was accepted into the National Ballet Company as a member of the *corps de ballet*. She celebrated this new triumph by buying a dozen almond cookies from her favourite neighbourhood bakery, and eating them all at once.

Chapter 5
A Year in the Corps

classical ballet company is divided into three ranks. The most celebrated dancers are the principal dancers, or prima ballerinas, as they are sometimes known. The principal dancers occupy the leading roles in ballets such as *Giselle* or *Swan Lake*, and they receive most of the public attention. Just below them are the soloists, who dance supporting roles and solo variations within a ballet. The largest group is the *corps de ballet*. As the lowest-ranking dancers, they are responsible for the large group formations and crowd scenes in most classical works.

While Karen was thrilled to be a professional dancer, the corps wasn't all it was cracked up to be. Taller than most of the other corps members, Karen was regularly relegated to the back of the stage, where her only job was to look the same as everybody else. This was next to impossible for someone who had the talent to become one of the world's leading prima ballerinas. But at only 20 years of age, Karen Kain had much to learn, and her education would cover more than just ballet steps. While a principal dancer may only appear in one or two productions, corps members in those days danced in every piece in a season, and frequently in up to eight performances per week. The corps members earned a weekly salary of only $80. The lack of time for a social life was a blessing in disguise — they couldn't afford one anyway.

In one of Karen's first rehearsals, the corps was learning a sequence from *Swan Lake*. The swans were to move across the stage in two diagonal lines, intersecting and crossing in the middle. It was simple enough, although with 24 swans, it got a little chaotic. The trick was for everyone to start on the same leg and to maintain the same rhythm. Easy enough, Karen thought. Start on the left. The women waiting on the sidelines crowded into the corners of the studio. Karen stood near the back, shoved between an ancient upright piano and several wardrobe crates.

Celia signalled the accompanist, and the lyrical music began. The dancers started moving in a slow, stately line, each dancer stepping with her left foot first. The rhythm was unhurried and calm. Karen nodded her head as the line of dancers cleared the way in front of her. It was her turn to start. She prepared, leading with her arms gracefully out front as she stepped onto the imaginary stage. "Stop," Celia called. The room fell silent, and the dancers stood in their places, looking at each other. "Left foot, Karen. Left foot."

Clapping her hands, Celia called out, "From the top." Karen nodded and apologized as the dancers gathered back into their respective corners. How could I have started on the wrong foot? Karen thought. This time, she was focused and ready. Left foot, left foot, she repeated to herself. But when her turn came, she started with the right foot again. "Miss Kain. Do you literally have two left feet?" Celia asked. The dancers tittered as Karen looked down and mumbled, "No." They began again. Karen knew she had to get it right this time. When her turn came, her heart was pounding in her ears and she got so flustered by wanting to get it right, that she mixed up her feet again.

Celia stood up and everything went silent. She walked the length of the studio, stopping in front of Karen. Celia reached over and viciously pinched the flesh of Karen's left thigh, twisting as she pinched. Karen gasped. Her leg stung; it would bruise later that night. Celia looked up at Karen haughtily, her eyebrows raised. She turned and walked back to the front of the studio. "Again," Celia said. Karen never started on the wrong leg again.

Celia ran the company according to old-school traditions. Her leadership was marked by inspiring fear in her dancers. She tolerated little, and had a reputation for exploding in a rage at mistakes made onstage. She and Betty alike had no time for expressions of sensitivity or frustration, which, in the case of the predominantly female ballet world, usually amounted to tears. Both knew that great achievement required great sacrifice. And both had put in Herculean effort toward their own dance careers. As a result, they had no patience for the frustrations of 20-year-old novices.

And Karen had her fair share of growing pains during her first years with the company. Her first performance with the National Ballet was in Roland Petit's *Kraanerg*, a relatively new piece of contemporary choreography. Her introduction to the supposedly glamorous world of professional dance began in the rehearsals. She was paired with a male dancer who had earned the nickname "The King of Garlic." He clearly enjoyed pungent foods and didn't feel it necessary to wash his dance clothing with much frequency. At a certain point in the ballet, Karen and her odorous partner had to lie curled up together for almost five minutes. Karen managed to inhale some fresh air now and again, but eventually was forced to speak to the ballet master. Her partner promptly cleaned up his act.

The comedy continued well into the performance. During the costume fitting, Karen mentioned that her white unitard was a little tight. The crotch was nearly five inches too low! "It's fine," the harried wardrobe mistress snapped. Not wanting to draw attention to her height anyway, Karen slunk off with her costume. On the very first entrance of her professional debut, the choreography included a large side

Karen Kain in *Solitaire* (1969)

split. In executing this move, Karen gave the audience more than they'd bargained for. Her costume ripped back to front! Karen learned a very important lesson about costume altera- tions, and about speaking up.

A Year in the Corps

The learning curve was steep as a new professional. In her second production, George Balanchine's *The Four Temperaments*, Karen froze as soon as she hit the stage. All of the choreography and previous months of rehearsal were forgotten. Miserable and panic-stricken, she flailed through the piece half a beat behind and copying everyone else.

Every season, the National Ballet would perform across Canada and the United States everywhere from large centres to tiny, backwater towns. In the early 1970s, touring on a small budget meant buses and roadside motels, not first-class air travel. On the first morning of Karen's first tour, the dancers filed onto the bus, still rumpled from sleep. Their bags had been tossed into a pile haphazardly beside the bus and the haggard driver struggled to cram them all in the baggage compartment beneath. Celia arrived a few minutes later, and immediately dragged two of the male dancers off the bus to help. Even that early in the morning, she looked perfectly composed. She took her seat at the front, folded her coat in her lap, and as the bus rolled out of the parking lot, Karen couldn't help but feel homesick already.

By the time they arrived in Red Bank, New Jersey, at 5:00 p.m., the dancers were sure they couldn't perform. Their hips were stiff from sitting all day in the cramped bus, and their backs were aching. Groaning, they piled out and retrieved their bags. They were staying at a dismal motel by the highway, with a neon sign that buzzed loudly the whole night.

The dancers gathered for an onstage warm-up at 6:00 p.m., having to fit dinner in somewhere between checking into the motel and finding their way to the theatre. There was just one dressing room to be shared between the men and women, with only a narrow curtain for privacy. Two bare bulbs hung gloomily from the ceiling. Several wardrobe boxes were strewn about and a chipped mirror leaned against the wall. Karen shook her head and looked down ... the floor was covered in an inch of ice-cold water!

After the performance, the dancers went to an all-night truck-stop diner for something to eat; this became a common occurrence while on tour. By the time Karen got to bed, it was nearly midnight, and the bus would be leaving the next morning promptly at 9:00. The 50 company dancers shared hotel rooms, dressing rooms, and cramped buses for as long as four months at a time. Tempers ran high in such close quarters, and the working conditions proved to be no better. This tour visited every small town in the American Midwest, and by the time it was over, Karen had reached her limit. If this is what life in the company is like, I'm just not up for it, she thought.

After the first season ended, Karen went abroad for a brief period of study in London and Paris. There, she made a decision: if her second season with the National Ballet wasn't more challenging than the first, she would find another line of work. That autumn, Peter Wright created a contemporary ballet in Toronto called *The Mirror Walkers.* The four principal roles had been cast, but when one dancer decided to take a year off, Wright auditioned three dancers for the role: a principal dancer, a soloist, and Karen, who was just a lowly member of the corps. Karen got the part. Despite resentment from other dancers, Karen relished the opportunity to really perform. Unfortunately, when the show was over, she was relegated back to the corps.

Undaunted, she knocked on Celia Franca's office door. She entered timidly, but within minutes she had blurted, "Oh, Miss Franca, can I learn one of the solo parts?" Celia looked at her with a small smile and after a moment asked, "How would you like to learn the Swan Queen?" The Swan Queen is one of the most coveted roles in classical ballet — the major part in *Swan Lake*, and a challenging one at that. "The what?" Karen asked in disbelief. Celia had already dismissed any protest. "The Swan Queen," she said, looking down to the papers at her desk. "We'll start soon." She didn't look back up until Karen had practically stumbled out of her office.

Chapter 6
The Gold Dust Twins

One day after company class, Betty Oliphant stopped Karen in the hallway. "Want to see the next Erik Bruhn?" she whispered conspiratorially. The two women rushed down the hall to the next studio, where a men's class was going on. Wearing black leotards and standing in lines, the men took off in unison, turning in the air. Karen peeked in through a crack in the door then looked back at Betty, confused. Surely she didn't mean the skinny boy with glasses? Betty nodded, barely able to contain herself. "He has chipmunk cheeks," was all Karen could manage.

Frank Augustyn was born in Hamilton to a family of German and Polish descent. His father, a steelworker, had modest hopes for his two sons, but when Frank's interest in gymnastics turned into a love of dance, he was angry. Fiercely masculine in nature, Frank's father couldn't understand his son's interest in something reserved if not for women, than for men of questionable character. His life was about hard, physical labour and raising a family. What his father didn't understand was that hoisting grown women above your head all day *was* hard physical labour. Frank would struggle in his chosen career throughout his life. He would struggle against the perceptions of the outside world, which generally assumes that all male dancers are homosexual, and also against the same beliefs from the dance world. Frank would endure inappropriate advances from some of the most famous male dancers in the world. But in the late 1960s, he was simply an innocent young man pursuing a dream — to become a dancer.

Karen didn't take much notice of young Frank, who still wore glasses and was rather skinny in his first year with the company. They were partnered together for the demanding *Intermezzo*, choreographed by Eliot Feld in 1971. Feld was well-respected in the ballet world, and this was a fantastic opportunity for the young dancers. Right from the beginning, however, there were problems. "You're self-indulgent, Karen," was the first comment out of Feld's mouth in rehearsal. They had barely learned the first section's steps and Karen was trying to feel the movement in the music, suspending the slow movements that seemed carried by the song. Stunned, she looked at Frank, who moved a little closer as though protecting her. Karen was not Feld's only target, though. Somehow, he managed to verbally attack all of the dancers, zeroing in on what they felt were their strengths.

Karen was mortified. She stayed late into the night after rehearsal, practising the complicated waltz step. She repeated it over and over. When she finally went to bed that evening, she was sure she had it. Little did she realize that partnering in ballet has as much give and take as a real-life relationship. The next morning, Frank had completely for-gotten that section's choreography. Terrified and angry, Karen hissed, "Don't you remember this?"

Frank shrugged and grinned. "No, I'm sorry, I don't," he said.

Karen sighed and looked over her shoulder. Luckily, Eliot was working with another couple on a lift. Karen showed Frank the waltz step. He still couldn't get it. Again, she showed him, this time a little slower. Still not right. The third time, Karen rushed through the steps: waltzing left and right, turning and leaping with tiny steps. Frank tried to follow, but her pace was too fast. His feet got confused under him and the sudden changes in direction were too quick to follow. They both fell to the floor on top of each other. Eliot stopped and everyone looked over. Karen bolted to her feet, blushing. She shot Frank a look; he just grinned and shrugged. "Sorry," he said.

Frank's best qualities as a dancer were his natural strength and musical sense. He would never learn the steps as quickly as Karen, but was always popular because of his great sense of humour. Frank brought levity to a world that took itself too seriously.

A couple of months later, Karen was to dance her first Juliet with another dancer, Laszlo Surmeyan. An experienced and competent dancer, Laszlo's guidance had helped Karen get through her first *Swan Lake*, and she was confident that her debut in Romeo and Juliet would go just as well. Several days before the opening, Laszlo twisted his knee landing from a sweeping *tour en l'air* — a turning leap that lands in a lunge. Karen saw his leg bend unnaturally as he landed, and her stomach fell. She knew he wouldn't be dancing. Celia scanned her cast lists the next day and called Frank in for the 9:00 a.m. rehearsal. There were only three days left until the opening, and both Frank and Karen knew that learning steps didn't come quickly for him.

There was no time for theatrics or frustration; Frank had to learn Romeo's routine and fast. The pair worked steadily for almost 12 hours that day, breaking only for short meals. They ate quickly, talking intently about the steps and various sequences. They left at 10:00 that night, and returned to the studio at 7:00 the next morning. By noon, Karen's nerves were frazzled. Frank was having trouble with one of the sections. They went over it and over it. Frank shook his head and stepped back. Karen sat down, put her hands to her head and tried to fight the tears. She couldn't. She looked up at the clock; there were only 36 hours left until curtain. "We're not going to make it," she said, beginning to sob.

"Hey," Frank said, kneeling down close. He squeezed her shoulder. "We'll do it." He hugged her briefly and got up. He began to dance the section in jest, moving with his back bent unnaturally and his arms and hands curled into gnarled-looking stumps. "See, no problem," he said. He looked like an orangutan, clowning through one of classical ballet's most revered dances. Karen laughed, shook her head, and got up. Frank bounded over and picked her up over his head. He spun her around and then put her under his arm as though dragging her back to his cave. She pounded his back, breathless with laughter. Frank put her down and smiled at her. He touched her face.

Karen and Frank's partnership was marked by these dynamics for the next several years: she was high-strung and obsessive; he was laid-back and calm. While the combination was sometimes explosive — the two would get into screaming matches so intense that they had to be physically restrained sometimes — it also balanced each of them out. Frank soothed Karen's anxiety and she pushed him to improve as a performer.

Life at the National Ballet Company was cloistered; dancers arrived for class at 9:00 each morning, ate lunch together, rehearsed together, and performed together, and nights without performances were usually filled with social activities. Men and women were thrown together in this environment, but they were seldom alone. As time went on, Karen began to notice Frank as a man who had outgrown his chipmunk cheeks. He was a man of incredible strength and musicality. He was a man with a wonderful sense of humour and a warm heart. Frank, too, began to see Karen in a different light. It seemed the more they worked together, the more they learned about the person behind the work.

In 1972, Celia was invited to judge a new but prestigious competition in Moscow. The first Moscow International Ballet Competition had taken place in 1969, when a young and virtually unknown Mikhail Baryshnikov won for male solo. Since then, the event had become known for introducing young talent to the ballet world. Celia took two of her dancers aside one afternoon, and told them it was time. Frank and Karen had only two weeks to prepare two new and challenging pieces. The competition was highly political — the judges were known to favour the Russian dancers, and Celia would have very little influence on the outcome. To top it off, Russian stages are built on a rake, or slant, making them higher at the back and very difficult to dance on. Russian ballet dancers trained and worked on these stages every day; Frank and Karen had only two weeks to learn.

The production crew of the National Ballet built a small version of the slanted stage, but it was only large enough to stand on. They fumbled through some lifts and turns, but it was impossible to get a sense of the real thing. They'd have to rely on their rehearsals in Moscow. But upon arriving, the pair's underdog status didn't improve. Drawing the short straw for rehearsal times, their only rehearsal was scheduled for 1:00 a.m., the same day of their first performance.

Life in Russia in the early 1970s was very difficult. Food was scarce and its quality unpredictable. The two dancers rapidly lost weight — and therefore energy — in these conditions. Decent food was virtually impossible to find, and they had only brought orange-flavoured juice crystals with them.

After little success in finding food at their hotel, Frank and Karen ventured out to try some of Moscow's restaurants. They walked into a plush restaurant off Red Square that had been recommended by the Canadian ambassador. The waiter arrived, and Karen muddled through some of her phrasebook Russian to order sausages, onions, and cheese. The waiter shook his head. "*Nyet*," he said. Flustered, Karen tried something else, asking for cured ham and pickled beets. *Nyet.* She pointed at the menu. *Nyet.* And pointed again. *Nyet.* Finally, she told the waiter to bring whatever they did have. Apparently, just because a restaurant had a menu didn't necessarily mean they had the items listed on it. The waiter returned after what seemed like an eternity with a plate of bread, butter, and sturgeon.

The next day at the same restaurant, Karen lucked out — her first choice was chicken soup, and it was available! When it arrived, a tiny chicken wing floated in the grey broth, feathers and all. Karen started to laugh, but in her fatigue and hunger, the laughing quickly turned into tears.

Celia had been all but sequestered away. She had no idea what Karen and Frank were going through. As a judge, she had far more luxurious accommodation and sustenance. The day of their first and only rehearsal, she saw how gaunt and pale her young protégés had become, so she smuggled them into her hotel. She had proper food brought in, and later that evening she encouraged them to get some rest. Celia led Karen and Frank to her room, which had two single beds. "Now, you two darlings just rest for an hour," she said, locking the door behind her so they wouldn't be disturbed. Karen and Frank had never been locked in a room together before. The door closed behind them, and they stared at each other. The combination of good food, stress, and hormones seemed to galvanize in that moment. Two years of partnership and friendship transformed instantly into passion. When Celia returned an hour later, she found the two of them "sleeping" in separate beds, not noticing the steamed windows and Karen's unruly hair.

Moscow audiences were nothing like the polite and quiet North American crowds. They were loud and judgmental, both in their support and their disapproval. On the first day of the competition, Karen and Frank waited backstage, trying to peek through the curtains at both the audience and the dancer before them. The house was packed and the audience boisterous. A young Japanese ballerina walked onstage and began her variation. Technically, she danced very well, executing her turns and steps with precision. But she looked very nervous. She kept looking down instead of out at the crowd, and the audience seemed to sense it. It was as though they could smell her fear. The crowd began to whisper.

Their voices grew louder and louder, peppered now and again with a snicker. The Japanese ballerina began to panic, and faltered on an easy step. The audience roared with laughter. She blinked quickly, and Karen could see from the wings that her hands were shaking. She looked as though she was going to cry, which made everything worse. She landed a jump poorly, having to catch herself with her other foot, and a tear spilled down her cheek. Again, more laughter. She tried to keep dancing as she sobbed, but the crowd was openly mocking her now, making loud crying noises, and laughing. The dancer stood still for a long moment, trying to regain her composure, but it was no good. Accompanied by peals of laughter, she turned and walked off stage. The curtain dropped and Karen and Frank looked at each other.

No one at the competition had really heard of the Canadian dancers, so theoretically they had nothing to lose. The young country hadn't yet produced any artists known at an international level, and Karen and Frank saw this event as their chance. As the curtain rose, the audience gasped at the sight of the handsome young couple in their strange and elaborate costumes. They began to move, and it was as though they could do no wrong. Karen's *arabesques* were accompanied by oohs and aahs. Frank's high, powerful leaps, a more challenging variation than was common (thanks to their coach Rudolf Nureyev), were rewarded with explosions of cheers. Moscow loved them!

The couple sailed through that first round, only to find out that it was not graded. Their more challenging — and less rehearsed — dances were yet to come. They made it through the second round, dancing Roland Petit's *Le Loup*, a showcase for Frank. The third round left eight couples, and by some strange coincidence, they were all dancing the same piece! They were dancing the *Black Swan pas de deux*, but the Canadians' interpretation was different than the native Bolshoi Ballet's, using different movements and a different score. The Bolshoi orchestra, of course, didn't know their specific version. And, it got worse. Karen and Frank were slated last.

Backstage they listened to the same music repeated over and over. They listened to the audience applaud the same tricks. The applause lessened with every new couple. Hours later, when the Canadians were finally called, the audience cheered loudly. But, once their program was announced, the cheer turned into a collective groan. This was the eighth time that day the audience had seen this dance, and the eighth time the orchestra had played the score. The couple squeezed each other's hands as the curtain rose, determined to do the best they could. Sensing the audience's distaste (and probably wanting to get the piece over with), the orchestra's conductor set the tempo twice as fast as Frank and Karen had rehearsed. Karen jumped and twirled, leaping with strength and grace despite the impossible speed. Frank held her tightly during her spins, expertly manoeuvring Karen on the drastically slanted stage. The pair flew through the dance, operating on pure instinct. Despite the gasps of awe at their performance, the pair left the stage utterly crushed. They were sure they had failed.

Celia's position at the competition meant she couldn't even console her dancers. The judges were locked away in the depths of the Bolshoi Theatre. Exhausted, Karen and Frank slowly packed up their things backstage and prepared to slink back to their hotel. They heard the other dancers whispering in the dressing rooms. They heard the Russian dancers chattering with certainty in their voices, sounding as though they knew they would win.

Celia called early the next morning. Not surprisingly, the Russians had taken 16 of the 23 prizes. But Celia also had some good news. Frank had placed seventh in the men's division, and Karen had taken silver in the women's. The biggest coup had been their first dance, the *Bluebird pas de deux*. It hadn't counted for marks, but nevertheless, it had been awarded the prize for best *pas de deux*! Moscow's media splashed the victories all over the newspapers and television, but it was nothing compared to what they'd find when they got home.

On the flight back to Canada, Karen slept while Frank gazed out the window at the lights of Reykjavik, Iceland. A few hours into their journey, the flight attendant came down the aisle to hand Frank a note. As she stood by, he opened the envelope. He had to read it twice. Canadian prime minister Pierre Trudeau and his wife had invited Frank and Karen for cocktails and dinner at Sussex Drive that evening. Frank tried to act as though this sort of thing happened every day, saying he'd have to consult with Karen. When the flight attendant moved farther down the aisle, he jostled Karen awake. Karen, of course, was thrilled, but the unexpected stop in Ottawa meant their luggage would go on to Toronto without them. "We can't go to dinner at the prime minister's dressed like this," Karen cried.

They arrived in Ottawa and went straight to the hotel. With only an hour to spare, Karen and Frank had to buy clothing from the shop in the hotel's lobby. The dress waiting for Karen was terribly tacky, covered in large bright flowers, and Frank's outfit was an all-beige pantsuit that made him look ridiculous. Both outfits were way too big and had to be safety-pinned in place! But what they were wearing didn't matter. It felt like a dream for Karen to be ushered in through the huge oak doors and find a line of people, including the prime minister of Canada, waiting to meet her. Pierre Trudeau walked over to her, smiling. She could barely speak as she shook his hand. He put his arm around her and led her through the line, introducing her to his wife, visiting dignitaries, and Canadian politicians. A glass of champagne was thrust in her hand and as though through a fog, she heard the prime minister congratulating them on their incredible contribution to Canadian culture. She looked around, and pinched herself, but it still didn't seem real.

Arriving in Toronto the next morning, Karen and Frank were shocked to discover that they had become stars. John Fraser, a dance critic for *The Globe and Mail*, had covered the Moscow competition round by round, holding the Canadian public's attention with a fervour normally reserved for the Stanley Cup playoffs. By the time Frank and Karen returned home, they were famous.

Despite Karen's shyness with the media, she would soon become a household name, thanks to journalist John Fraser. He had been hired as a music critic for the *Toronto Telegraph* in 1970. In the beginning, he covered dance because he had to; it was part of the job. He'd had no interest in dance, but after attending several seasons of the National Ballet Company, he was converted. As a new balletomane (as ballet fans are called), he was surprised to see how little media attention ballet received in Canada. By the early 1970s, it was Fraser's mission to get dance on the front page. He moved to *The Globe and Mail*, a larger national newspaper, and single-handedly introduced Canada to the world of ballet.

The timing of the Moscow competition was perfect. Canadians had enjoyed a growing sense of nationalism on the world's stage because of Expo '67, and skier Nancy Greene's 1968 Olympic gold medal. In 1971, Canada won the Canada–Soviet Union hockey series, which was followed the next year by the Moscow International Ballet Competition.

"Karen and Frank were like manna from heaven," John Fraser recalls. "All I had to do was celebrate them." Fraser covered the competition as closely as any sports series, and his build-up had readers in hysterics. He called them the Gold Dust Twins, implying that everything they touched turned to gold. Fraser's influence on the world of ballet would become more dramatic than ever by 1974, with Baryshnikov's sudden and dramatic defection in Toronto; but this was more than enough for Karen.

The morning after Frank and Karen returned from Moscow, Celia breezed into class as though nothing had changed. "Let us begin," she called into the room as the chaos of warm-up took the ordered shape of class, lines of dancers standing at the barre, poised and silent. The door squeaked open, breaking through this silence, and Karen mumbled an apology before taking her place at the barre. She was still jetlagged and feeling the effects of the previous night's champagne. Through the entire class, Celia didn't say a word to Karen, passing her by as she corrected the dancers to her left and right.

In rehearsal that afternoon, it was the same. Celia worked with a different couple, labouring through the steps of a new dance to be premiered in a few weeks. Karen and Frank were only understudies for this section and they worked in the back of the studio, imitating the other dancers' movements, straining to hear Celia's corrections.

There was a knock at the door, and one of the administrative girls apologetically tiptoed to the front of the studio. "Ms. Franca," she called. Celia sighed and walked over to the girl, who whispered rather frantically in her ear. Celia took her by the arm and led her out of the studio, slamming the door behind. Celia's muffled shouts came through the door, and the dancers looked at each other, shaking their heads and shrugging. She came back moments later, clearly flustered.

Ticket sales for the National Ballet of Canada had suddenly exploded after the Moscow Competition. People called in, wanting tickets for the nights Karen and Frank would perform, but in Celia's company, everyone was treated the same. If audience members came to see the company, they saw the entire company; she would never announce casting before a performance. But there was a deluge of phone calls, and the administration had to react. They sent someone down to the studio to find out Celia's casting decisions right away. She had no choice but to tell them.

Frank and Karen's performances sold out immediately, which left other nights under-attended. It didn't take long for the other company members to figure out the casting announcements. In fact, a quick scan through the morning paper would tell them who was scheduled to perform that night. Frank and Karen's partnership was only about one year old, and the two dancers were still very young; Frank was only 21, and Karen was 22. The other principal dancers felt unappreciated, especially since most of them were more experienced by several years! Class and rehearsals became very awkward as the resentment grew. The public had undermined Celia's democratic approach to the company, and there was nothing she could do about it.

Frank and Karen were swept away by the wave of attention. After their performances, they were held in 15-minute curtain calls, smiling until their cheeks hurt and gathering great heaps of flowers. Backstage, their dressing rooms were packed with strange people wishing them well. They tried to change out of the costumes with at least a shred of privacy. There was no time to remove their makeup as they were rushed out into the theatre lobby to be swarmed by more fans wanting autographs or photographs. Reporters and camera people crowded them, asking more questions than they could possibly answer.

Finally, after the lobby emptied out, Frank and Karen had time to retrieve their things from backstage. All the other dancers were gone by this time, leaving an eerie and reproachful silence behind. Next, they'd be swept away to a party hosted by a rich patron or politician. Karen was painfully shy and forced to make small talk with women three times her age, many asking her for the secret of staying so slim. Her champagne flute was filled after every sip and trays of fancy canapés were thrust under her nose. Opening-night parties would stretch into the early morning, and Karen could barely stay awake. She longed to be home in bed, surrounded by nothing but silence. Frank and Karen would usually slip out as inconspicuously as possible, hoping to catch a few hours of sleep before 9:00 class the next morning.

The pressure was intense. Privately, Karen and Frank felt they weren't as good as everyone believed. Dancers in the company were jealous of all the attention the two of them received; Karen and Frank weren't the only ones who felt it was unwarranted. Alienated by the company and thrown together by extreme circumstances, romance blossomed between them. It was Frank and Karen against the world, or so it seemed. It was the beginning of a love affair that would face many challenges over the next seven years.

The launch of Karen's ballet career began at the cusp of the 1970s. In 1973, she had only dipped her toes into the world of stardom with John Fraser's coverage of the Moscow Competition. At the competition, Roland Petit, the artistic director of the Ballet de Marseille, noticed Karen's burgeoning talent. He took one look at her during rehearsal and said loudly, "I must have her at Marseilles!" At that time, Canadians had barely heard of Karen and Frank, and hadn't yet seen them. But by the mid-1970s, they would be known in almost every Canadian household as the Gold Dust Twins.

Chapter 7
The Prima Ballerina

Karen was naturally timid, and her teachers would have to tell her to stop looking at the floor in class. Onstage, she was a different person, finding confidence in the characters she portrayed. Nothing could stop her from pushing herself toward excellence in each and every performance, and each and every role. Karen lived to dance, even though she didn't always know how to handle the fame that came along with it. "You'd better start wearing some makeup," was the only advice she got from Celia Franca.

Karen was about to be thrown into the limelight in ways she had never imagined, thanks to the world's most famous male dancer, Rudolf Nureyev. Nureyev was almost single-handedly responsible for Karen's international career, and for putting the National Ballet of Canada on the map. Although Karen was quite happy, and probably most comfortable within the cloisters of the National Ballet, Nureyev wouldn't let her talent be hidden from the world's stage. Together they danced all over the globe, from Vienna to London to Australia.

In 1973, Rudolf Nureyev, known internationally as one of the best, most charismatic male dancers in the world, came to work with the National Ballet — a major coup for Canada. Nureyev singled Karen out, and between 1973 and 1976, Karen juggled two of the finest male dancers of her time: Rudolf and Frank.

Rudolf was a Russian-born, Kirov-trained dancer who defected to North America in 1961, at the age of 23. He and his close friend, the Danish Erik Bruhn, took the dance world by storm. In doing so, they enhanced the status of the male dancer, or *danceur noble*. A great inspiration for male dancers around the world, including Frank Augustyn, Nureyev had the charisma, virtuosity, and smouldering good looks to capture audiences.

The role of men in the ballet world, and the status of male dancers among the general populace, is ambiguous at best. It was all the more so in the 1960s and 1970s. Male dancers are not only universally assumed to be gay, but dancing is certainly not considered to be a "manly" profession. Nureyev and Bruhn, and later Baryshnikov, elevated the status of the male dancer, whose function in dance had been merely carrying around the ballerina. They created a great appreciation for male dancers. More male solos were added to classical productions, and in recent years, all male pieces have been successfully choreographed. Male dancers usually display their incredible strength with powerful jumps, spinning leaps, and impressive feats of stamina. But for Frank, Nureyev's arrival was the beginning of a career that would be overshadowed by Karen, right from the beginning.

Nureyev's arrival also brought a new approach to the company, one that caused some rumblings with Celia. In its infancy, ballet as a form developed in two very different ways, separated by culture and geography. The British school was, unsurprisingly, known for its restraint, modesty, and precision. Indeed, British ballet has been criticized as being so academically focused on technique as to not even consider the audience. Journalist John Fraser once described a British-style dancer careening off stage after an intensely emotional variation and acting as though she had just finished her multiplication tables instead of performing a heart-wrenching love scene. The other predominant style was, in effect, the opposite of British subtlety. Russian ballet was big and dramatic; movements and gestures were approached with passion and gusto, and emotional expression was revered. The irony was that most Western European and North American dancers were trained from Russian-based systems, like Ceccheti. These systems were applauded for their technical purity and difficulty. However, when it came to performance, it was a different story.

Russian ballet went through several renaissances from the days of the rich ballet impresarios such as Sergei Diaghilev and his Ballets Russes to the opulent Imperial Ballet of the tsars. However, no political shift altered the world of ballet as much as the Soviet Revolution. Lenin's government severely cut subsidies to the Bolshoi and Kirov (then Mariinsky) Companies because of their "imperialist" repertory. As a result, classics such as *Carmen* were drastically altered to suit the Soviet's communist messages. For example, traditionally a Spanish seductress, Carmen was turned into a Jewish communist girl in Poland.

Under Soviet rule, and even afterwards, Russian ballet was subject to the same strict controls as the rest of society. Dancers who wanted artistic freedom, to perform as guest artists with foreign companies, create their own works, or become international performing stars (as in the case of Rudolf Nureyev) were forced to conform or defect. Defection meant separation from friends and family, insecure political status, and the likelihood of prosecution in their home country if they ever tried to return.

Nureyev defected in 1961, dramatically throwing himself into the arms of a pair of unsuspecting gendarmes at the Paris airport, while under KGB watch. He was granted political asylum, but the incident resulted in non-stop surveillance of the Kirov Company. Dancers were told to watch for signs of insubordination, such as arriving late for company meetings or hanging around with "undesirables." Suspect dancers were often banned from foreign tours. In fact, Nureyev himself was banned from several foreign tours early in his career. But those were reprimands for his temper, not his political fervour.

After Nureyev's departure, the male superstars of the Kirov were Yuri Soloviev and Mikhail (Misha) Baryshnikov. Tragically, Soloviev took his own life at the age of 37, ending what could have been a stellar international career. That left Baryshnikov as the Kirov's sole male star. The Russian company toured Europe and North America, but as was consistent with the politics, the dancers were under close watch at all times, and only permitted to perform government regulated dances.

The *Globe and Mail* dance critic John Fraser was working to deadline at 10:00 on a sultry June night in Toronto. The Kirov Company was in town and Baryshnikov was sending Toronto's O'Keefe Centre audiences into raptures. It was opening night, and Fraser had sped away from the O'Keefe Centre at intermission to get his review in for the next day's paper. He sweated as he typed, still hearing the music and seeing Misha's extraordinary elevation and powerful technique. Fraser had been a huge fan of the "big" male dancers ever since Nureyev came to work with the National Ballet. Fraser butt out another cigarette into his overflowing ashtray and choked back a sip of cold coffee. His phone rang and he answered with a distracted, "Fraser here." The voice on the other end sounded familiar. "Got a pen?" the voice asked. "Write this down."

Fraser was intrigued as he rifled through the piles of paper on his desk, searching for a clean sheet. He wrote down the cryptic details the caller dictated. "What is this about?" Fraser asked. "Take this to Baryshnikov tonight," the caller replied. "We'll give you the first interview; just keep this quiet." Before Fraser could say anything else, the line went dead. His head spinning, Fraser looked at his watch. He dashed off the last paragraph, filed the story, and sped out the door to deliver the message. He had met Misha a number of times before, interviewing him after this show or that, so they already had a good professional rapport.

When Fraser arrived backstage, he was breathless. One of the stagehands teased him as he let Fraser backstage. "What happened, Johnny? Forget your favourite pencil?" Fraser found Baryshnikov in his dressing room. Fraser poked his head in and said, "I have something for you." Misha ushered him in and closed the door. John handed him the note with the strange details. The dancer read it quickly, nodded, and then asked Fraser for a light. Baryshnikov burned the note in the dressing room sink, and thanked him before grabbing his things and leaving the theatre. Fraser was stunned.

Five days later, just moments after the final curtain fell on the Kirov's performance run, Baryshnikov bolted out the backstage door. He jumped into a waiting car driven by his friend Tim Stewart. He fled in the night to the Stewarts' cottage in the Caledon Hills, 40 minutes outside of Toronto. After a few days of confusion, a familiar voice came through on

Fraser's newsroom telephone. "Get your things. We're picking you up in five minutes," it said. A black car was waiting on the street and Fraser was taken to the hideaway cottage in the hills. John Fraser was given the exclusive first interview with the most famous defector in Canadian — and perhaps ballet's — history.

Fraser had become the voice of ballet in Canada at a time when dance writing and dance critics were as important as dance itself. During the 1960s and 1970s, publications such as the *Village Voice* in New York became the source of the newest critiques on art and performance, then a brand new field of research. Dance has always been a dark horse in performance criticism, often falling between the cracks of theatre and music. Journalists such as John Fraser have been essential for creating a dialogue about the art form. And, in the case of Baryshnikov's highly controversial defection, sometimes journalists became political activists.

While Baryshnikov's impact on Canada was generally political (he did most of his subsequent performing in the United States), Nureyev's impact was purely artistic. And no one felt his impact more deeply than Karen. Nureyev arrived in Toronto in 1972 to mount his production of *The Sleeping Beauty* with the National Ballet. It was well-known at the time that Nureyev was simply looking for a North American vehicle for his exploding solo career. Still, the National Ballet was happy to comply. At the time, it was a second-rate company, and Nureyev's influence would help take it to the next level.

In the first rehearsal, Nureyev sat at the front of the studio wearing his characteristic wool toque and warm-up clothing. He sipped tea as he watched the corps perform the fairy variations from the prologue. As he watched, he imagined jewelled costumes flashing in the stage lights as he re-choreographed the dances with far more difficult movements. "That should be double turn," he said over his shoulder to Celia, who nodded.

Karen moved to the front of the studio to perform the principal fairy's solo as the other fairies backed toward the side of the room. She moved so lightly, so lyrically, it looked to Rudolf as though the music was alive within her. Her steps were precise, and he could tell how much farther Karen could go. He knew it just by looking at her; she had star quality. Rudolf stood up suddenly, motioning for the accompanist to stop playing. He turned to Celia, one hand on his hip, one pointing at Karen. "Why is she not cast as Aurora?" he demanded in heavily accented English. Celia smiled tightly, as the entire company looked at Karen.

Celia walked over to Rudolf and put her arm around him. She whispered that Karen was a new company member and had received some lovely casting opportunities in other dances. "Ridiculous," Rudolf said. "She should be Aurora. Look at her. Princess!" Celia tried in vain to lead him out of the studio, telling him that they could discuss this in private at another time. "No, no. Is fine. Is fine," Rudolf said, sitting back down. "I will make her star next time. She will be my partner." He nodded as though it was all decided.

Meanwhile, Karen's stomach had dropped with excitement and terror. She stared, red-faced at the floor. The other dancers gaped at Karen with thinly veiled contempt. Celia seethed, and nodded at the accompanist to begin again. The female dancers weren't the only ones who felt singed by jealousy. Frank felt it, too. He and Karen had been together through everything. They were the Gold Dust Twins. What would happen now?

Rudolf's style was one of flash and flair. He would not shirk on the details, and insisted on dramatic jewellery, ornate costumes, and complicated sets. The budget for his production soared beyond the reach of the National Ballet. Celia met with the board members to figure out what to do. Celia had defended her choice to work with Nureyev amid grumbles of disapproval right from the start. Now the projected budget of $250,000 had grown to over $350,000, and the board was getting angry. Where were they going to find $100,000 at a moment's notice? "Figure it out," Celia snapped, before walking out of the meeting. Left without options, several board members had to re-mortgage their homes to make up the difference. They were not impressed.

This level of opulence was unheard of in Canadian ballet, and soon the media became interested. The opening night was a gala affair with the prime minister, the governor general, and other figures from Canadian high society in attendance. The reviews read more like accounting tables than aesthetic assessments. Fortunately, the investment paid off. The National Ballet was invited to engage in a 32-city North American tour, financed by dance impresario Sol Hurok, and culminating in a run at the prestigious New York Metropolitan Opera House.

Sol Hurok was born in the Ukraine, making his way to the United States almost penniless in the early 20th century. Hurok loved theatre, dance, and music. In his early years in New York, while working at a hardware store for a dollar a day, he stood at the back of the Hippodrome in Manhattan to watch Anna Pavlova, one of the first great ballerinas. After meeting her, he began presenting ballet acts in New York and all across the United States. In many ways, Hurok brought the world of ballet to America in the early 20th century, presenting the Ballets Russes, and eminent modern dancers such as Mary Wigman and Martha Graham. Later in his life, he was responsible for the incredible partnership of Rudolf Nureyev and British ballerina Margot Fonteyn.

While Karen and Frank were enjoying the beginnings of fame, Hurok was nearing the end of his life. Aged and in failing health, Hurok continued to go to the theatre to see the dancers warm up. It was a ritual he had begun many years ago. As Karen and Frank warmed up on stage at the Metropolitan Opera House, Hurok entered from the stage door off an alley behind the theatre. He leaned heavily on a cane as he shuffled down the aisle and sunk into one of the aisle seats. John Fraser, who sat behind him, leaned forward to introduce himself. Hurok nodded toward the stage, where Karen and Frank stood looking out into the seats. "They're stars, you know. Real stars," he said.

But Rudolph Nureyev was the man who would take Karen Kain from star to superstar. He finally got his wish to dance with Karen the following season as the National Ballet mounted its annual production of *Swan Lake*. Rudolf was an older, more experienced dancer who had partnered some of the finest ballerinas in the world, and Karen was his next choice. Karen was shy at first, and Rudolf's intense green eyes and smouldering sensuality so intimidated her that she could barely look him in the eyes during rehearsal.

Rudolf was very demanding, working almost harder than Karen herself. Rehearsals were all business, and Karen learned a lot. Rudolf was a showman, and he always demanded more from himself and his partners. Single pirouettes became doubles or triples, and everything had to be perfect. Karen practised and practised. Rudolf insisted on the best, and she was determined to give it.

The premiere performance of *Swan Lake* was in Montreal. That night, Karen felt on top of the world as she danced with Rudolf. Her limbs felt weightless, yet fiercely strong. The emotion of the tragic ballet burned in her chest. She felt connected to Rudolf, even from the opposite side of the stage. It was as though a magnet pulled them together. Rudolf felt it, too. That evening, Karen met Rudolf's gaze.

The ultimate goal in a dramatic performance is a state

Karen Kain and Rudolf Nureyev in *Les Sylphides* (1974)

of complete union, where the person you are in "real life" disappears, and you literally become someone else. Athletes experience this same sensation; they feel their bodies becoming one with the environment and the movement. Dance is a special combination of acting and athleticism, of emotional expression and movement. Some performances will feel physically perfect; some will feel expressively perfect. But to experience that ultimate combination, and to share that with someone else, is sublime.

A good partnership, much like a romantic relationship, has little to do with one individual choosing another. It is more like a chemical reaction between two dancers, a result far greater than the sum of its parts that brings out the best in each dancer. In a sort of magical synergy, these two dancers came together in an explosive, dynamic union that Canadian audiences had never seen before. As the curtain came down, Rudolf looked at Karen. "I knew you could do it," he said. "You and Margot [Fonteyn] have guts."

Karen and the rest of the National Ballet Company loved working with Rudolf. Frank, who incidentally looked like a younger Nureyev, emulated his style. Rudolf influenced Karen's career immensely, taking her along as he travelled around the world giving guest performance after guest performance. The company itself was honoured with a flood of invitations to tour all over the United States and Europe.

But Nureyev wasn't as appreciated outside the theatre. On July 27, 1975, the *New York Times* ran an article written by John Fraser with the blazing headline: "Nureyev, Leave Canadian Ballet Alone." Nureyev had brought his own aesthetic to the National Ballet, not to mention his opulence and obsession with international touring. His impact was generally seen as positive, but the shift in the ballet company wasn't as comfortable for some, including John Fraser. The Russian style is dramatically different from the more reserved British school, and as a British colony, Canada has long reflected the British reservation and decorum. The artistic impact of the United States is looked upon with similar mistrust. American aesthetics and culture are different from Canada's, and while the influence is mostly overlooked, sometimes it crosses an invisible cultural boundary.

Fraser saw the impact Nureyev was having on the company. Budgets were soaring, the dancing had changed, and their touring schedule meant they were out of the country more than they were in it. Canada had long fought for a truly national and independent ballet company, and now it was becoming impossible to distinguish the National Ballet of Canada from Rudolf Nureyev himself.

Chapter 8
The International Star

Dancers at the National Ballet received five weeks of holiday every year. In the dance company's beginning, it was difficult to keep the dancers employed on a full-time basis and they were laid off for two months every year. Dancers made very little money, so two months without pay was a struggle. Many of them used the time to perform elsewhere, acting as guest dancers with other companies.

In 1974, just as her career as an internationally known ballerina was beginning, Karen did her first guest performance with Roland Petit, the man who had once exclaimed, "I must have her for Marseilles!" Engagements with the Ballet de Marseille were booked between her performance commitments with the National Ballet for the next few years. She arrived in Marseilles in May, borrowing an apartment from a French dancer who was touring for the summer.

While ballet's style may change from country to country, the day-to-day life of a dancer is the same all over the world. Class came in Marseilles, as always, at 9:00 a.m. Karen found her way to the studios, housed in a building of enormous windows and breathtaking history. How many dancers had walked these halls before her? Class felt good after the long flight. Karen stretched her limbs in the familiar movements, getting ready for the next part of her career. She had never worked with another company before, and as nervous as she was, the change felt wonderful.

After class, a handsome dancer with dark hair walked over, introducing himself as Marcel. He had deep brown eyes, and Karen felt her stomach flip-flop when he repeated her name in his French accent. Flustered, she asked him where the rehearsal studios were. He offered to walk her down, so Karen gathered her things, and followed.

Working with Roland's company was entirely different than working at the National Ballet. The Ballet de Marseille was an exotic mix of dancers from all over the world, each with his or her own distinct style. The Ballet de Marseille was largely composed of men, most unheard of, and Roland preferred to bring in his *étoiles*, or female stars, as guests from all over the world. He moved with flourish, bursting into the studio, arms raised as though embracing the world. "Welcome to la belle Kain!" he gushed as he kissed Karen's cheeks. She blushed and said, "Hello Roland." Karen was in Marseilles just briefly this time, to perform in Roland's ballet *Le Loup*, a piece she and Frank had performed for the Moscow competition. They had three days of rehearsal before opening night.

Roland moved around the room sweeping his arms left and right as he described the production, and where this set piece or that curtain would be. He moved as he told the story of the ballet, dancing little phrases here and there. *Le Loup* was a tale of a man who was transformed into a wolf, and the young woman who grew to love him in his beastly form. "And this ... is your partner," Roland said, moving toward Karen with the handsome dark-haired man from class in tow. Karen blushed.

"Hello again," Marcel said.

Roland clasped his hands to his chest, "Ah, they have already met!" He raised his eyebrows and growled suggestively at the two dancers before moving away to begin rehearsal.

After rehearsal, Marcel invited Karen to dinner with some of the other company members. They went to a small café off a side street. They laughed and talked over a lovely meal and several bottles of red wine. After dinner, he drove her home on his motorbike. "Until tomorrow," he said, kissing her hand. Karen walked up the steps to her borrowed flat, floating on a cloud. The days passed in a blur, and Karen had never felt happier. Working with Roland was wonderful; he made her feel like she was perfect. Dancing with Marcel was distractingly delicious. She felt a special thrill holding onto his muscular arms as he lifted her.

Karen dined with a group of company dancers every night after rehearsal or performance. But when she arrived at the restaurant on one particular night, Marcel sat alone at the table. Karen sat down, feeling her stomach flip. "Where is everyone?" she asked.

"I wanted to be alone with you, Karen," Marcel said. He reached across the table and took her hand. Karen felt light-headed and terribly confused. Marcel was handsome and charming and wonderful — but what about Frank? The candle-lit café, the sweet smells of Marseilles, and the sounds of tinkling glasses were intoxicating. He reached over and pulled her face toward his.

The performances of *Le Loup* were very well received. France loved Karen; for most of the 1970s she would be known in France as La Kain. But she was due in Vienna for a performance with Rudolf, and after that, the National Ballet's season began. She could still hear the echoes of applause from the last curtain call as she quickly shoved her things into a duffle bag. In a rush, she had smeared cold cream on her face, trying to get most of the stage makeup off before leaving the theatre. A ring of pancake makeup still clung to the underside of her chin, and her eyes were still darkened from the mascara. Quickly kissing several dancers goodbye, she hurried out of the dressing room.

Marcel waited for her in the hallway. They embraced. "Come back soon to me, Karen," he implored. She nodded, wiping a tear away. He sighed and let her pass down the hall toward the exit. "Au revoir, Roland," she called down the hallway behind her. "Merci!" She pushed through the heavy metal door into the alley, where a black car sat idling. She got in, slammed the door, and sped off to the airport.

Karen arrived in Vienna at 2:00 a.m. and reached her hotel an hour later. She flopped into bed, falling into a black sleep for a few hours before getting up for morning class. Then there was rehearsal in the afternoon. And there was a performance after that. She hurried into class, finding her place at the barre beside dancers she'd never met. Karen was very relieved to see Rudolf, who rushed over to her, kissing her hello. Tonight, they would appear in *Swan Lake* at the Vienna State Opera. The afternoon was filled with rehearsal in the theatre. Every theatre is different, with unique wings and trap doors, and a dance is slightly different in every space it's performed. Every version is also unique, with a choreographer's particular timing and interpretation. Karen moved through these rehearsals as though in a dream. She felt separated from herself, somehow distant. She returned to the hotel to rest for an hour and have a meal. It felt as though no time had passed when, at 6:30, she was back at the theatre warming up onstage with the other dancers.

The performance went well. The audience held them in a 20-minute standing ovation. Rudolf was happy, and made a point of telling her so. He invited her out with the entourage of friends he seemed surrounded by in every city. Karen smiled, looked down, and told him she was just too tired. Leaning against the elevator wall, her body felt like lead. She opened her hotel room door to find the room filled with flowers. It was magical. From her ornately carved window, she could see the beautifully lit streets of Vienna.

Sitting down on the bed, she mused. Working with Rudolf, much like working with Roland, made Karen feel wonderful. Away from the cloisters of the National Ballet she felt free and confident, as though she could do anything. But, was this to be her life? Flying from one city to the next, living out of a suitcase and a hotel room, and barely getting to know the other dancers onstage? She hardly remembered her performance that night ... did she even deserve these flowers? She was lost in thought. When she woke up the next morning, she was still fully dressed, right down to her shoes.

Karen returned to Toronto a week later to perform with the National Ballet for the first half of the season. Things with Frank were strained. Karen became distant, thinking about Marcel constantly. "Karen, what is it?" Frank asked one evening when Karen was nearly silent over dinner in a downtown café. She looked across the table at Frank, his eyebrows knitted together in concern. She hated the thought of hurting him.

"Frank," she said, reaching across the table. "I'm in love with someone else." Frank exhaled slowly and leaned back in his chair. He could hear the blood pounding in his head. It felt like there was a rock in his stomach, but for some reason, he wasn't surprised. Karen had seemed different since she returned from Europe. Her friends had been looking at him strangely these days, and it seemed as though they knew something he didn't. Frank sat in silence for a long while, as Karen wept at the opposite end of the table. She looked so far away.

Frank got up and squeezed Karen's shoulder. "See you tomorrow," he said. He paid their bill and walked out into the chilly autumn air.

Between productions at the National Ballet, Karen returned to Marseilles again and again to star in ballets performed at the famous Paris Opera. In the late autumn of 1974, Karen went back to Marseilles to create the role of Albertine for Roland's *Les Intermittences du Coeur*. She ran through the airport to embrace Marcel, and it felt like she had never left. He threw her bag onto the back of his motorcycle, handed her a helmet, and sped into the city.

Karen's weeks in Marseilles were like a dream. He took her through France and in this idyllic, romantic setting, they fell in love. Their onstage partnership was excellent, and again, somehow, it made their off-stage relationship that much richer. Karen had never experienced this kind of passion before. With Frank, it had been a working relationship that sweetened to friendship and then to romance over time. Their romance was one of youth and hormones, but this new relationship felt much different. Leaning against the sea wall with the wind whipping through their hair, Marcel and Karen spoke of marriage.

Only a few short weeks later, Karen had to return to Canada. "Leave the National," Marcel pleaded. But she couldn't. The National Ballet of Canada was where her heart was. Karen had travelled back and forth for about a year when she finally realized that she couldn't marry Marcel. It was a romantic dream. A dream that was lovely amid the romance of Marseilles. Still, it was a dream that couldn't survive the real-life pressures of an international touring artist.

When she returned to Toronto, things felt much different. Karen would still perform with the Ballet de Marseille, but her romance with Marcel was over. They would remain good friends as the years passed, but Karen was learning the harsh lessons of a life in ballet — the touring, the loneliness, and the choices one makes to excel in this art form.

On her first morning back in Toronto, she arrived early to class, finding peace in the old familiarity of the Maitland Street studios. She stretched alone at the barre, feeling her own history coming through the walls and up through the floor. She had grown up here; she belonged here. The halls grew busier as the clock arms moved toward 9:00. Frank came into the studio and threw his bag in the corner. He saw Karen warming up and stood still, not quite sure what to do. Karen rushed over and held Frank close. "I've missed you," she said.

Frank returned her embrace. "I missed you, too," he said.

The National Ballet's dancers began pouring in to begin class. As they entered, they welcomed Karen back, some stopping to hug her in greeting. Things felt different this morning, Karen thought as she took her place at the barre. She felt like she was home.

But the feeling wouldn't last long. Two months in Toronto rehearsing a new season passed in a flash; then she was back overseas performing again. John Fraser had moved on from dance and was now working as the Chinese correspondent for *The Globe and Mail.* Unable to completely leave the dance world behind, he arranged for Karen and Frank to join him in Beijing for a cultural exchange. And so, between one closing night and the next opening, Karen flew off to China. She took special joy in teaching classes of young girls the international language of dance. She would invite them after class to her dressing room, where she taught stage makeup. Helping one girl with her eyeliner, she suddenly remembered herself at that age, 10 or 11 years old, full of hope and wonder at the glamorous life of a ballerina. Karen didn't have the heart to dispel the fantasy. But as she sat cramped in a coach seat crossing the Atlantic Ocean for the 20th time that year, she thought about how much those young dancers had yet to learn.

The chaos of Karen's career peaked in the autumn of 1976. Amid accepting honorary degrees and dining with everyone from the prime minister to Prince Charles, she undertook two simultaneous Canadian tours with both the

National Ballet and Petit's company. The National was moving through Canada west to east, and the Ballet de Marseille was travelling in the opposite direction. Karen flew back and forth crossing the country almost daily during the entire fall season. As a result, she was unable to maintain the regular rehearsal schedule with the National Ballet due to awkward flight times and performances with Petit. She soon started to feel the growing resentment from the other dancers and the administration.

On one such occasion, Karen stopped to pick up a magazine in the Toronto airport, missing her 7:00 a.m. flight to St. John's. The next flight wasn't until noon, and in a panic, she called her parents. They arrived to keep her company and calm her down — her life was so tightly scheduled that a simple mistake like this one could throw off the entire balance. She made it on the second flight, but the plane was unable to land in St. John's due to thick fog.

After a forced landing on a small airstrip in Gander, Newfoundland, and a painfully silent five-hour ride crammed in the back of a cab with four businessmen, Karen arrived in St. John's at 3:00 in the morning. She was exhausted during her performance of *Coppelia* with the National Ballet. She barely had time to sleep for a few hours before getting on a plane headed for Calgary. Karen was scheduled to perform that night with Petit's company, but her flight was delayed again due to fog. She landed in Calgary, only 90 minutes before the curtain went up.

She begged Roland to let her understudy perform instead. "We can't," he said. "The theatre is sold out for you." Karen began to sob uncontrollably as she started applying her makeup. She was exhausted, stressed, and felt more like a broken doll than Carmen, the passionate seductress she was just about to dance. Karen could barely think, so she gave into her instincts and let them carry her. Miraculously, it was one of her best performances. The ovation seemed to go on forever.

At the same time, things were falling apart in Toronto. The National Ballet was in turmoil. The rivalry between Celia Franca and Betty Oliphant developed sometime in the 1970s, but is largely mysterious. It is frequently referred to, but no one really knows how it began or why.

Celia ran "her" company with an iron fist. She had created the National Ballet essentially from the ground up, and she wanted no outside influence or meddling from the board of directors. She was very difficult to work with, known for walking out of board meetings, and shouting at administrative staff. Celia demanded complete obedience, which worked with her dancers, but wasn't as well received by the board. Fights over budgets and touring schedules reached impasse after impasse. Eventually, the board members were unable to work with Celia. In 1972, dancer David Haber was appointed as co-artistic director with Celia. Everyone hoped that David would be able to act as a mediator between Celia and the board. But by 1974, the rivalry between Betty and

Celia had reached a breaking point. The women became openly critical of one another, and Betty was open in sharing her opinion: she wanted Celia out. David, who was stuck in an impossible situation, was unable to make anybody happy. Decisions just came to a halt.

Rudolf's expectations were no easier to meet, and to make things worse, he was known for his moods and unpredictable temper. It was the National Ballet's final performance of *Sleeping Beauty* in New York. Late in the second act, the stage lights went out, leaving the stage in complete darkness. Normally, a spotlight would shine onto Rudolf, who was playing the role of the prince. At that point in the ballet, he was supposed to climb the castle stairs on his way to find the sleeping princess. If the spotlight technician was late or slightly off, Rudolf would normally snap his fingers. That night, however, it did not work. The technician missed the cue entirely, and Rudolf cursed audibly and stomped off stage. In the darkness, there was a loud clatter as the temperamental dancer kicked a steel lighting stand, bringing it crashing down. He tried to slap the stage manager across the face, and then stormed off backstage.

Meanwhile, Karen the princess feigned a peaceful sleep onstage. Other dancers surrounded her, also pretending to slumber. One by one, the dancers began to rustle nervously. Then Karen began to hear whispers. "He's not coming, Karen," someone whispered. Beginning to panic, Karen racked her brain — the sleeping princess can't possibly wake up on her own! Suddenly, from a completely different entrance, Nureyev stomped back onstage, made a false gesture of bending toward the princess, and produced a loud, mocking kissing noise. Karen "awoke" to two green eyes blazing in anger.

But Rudolf had kissed her too early. In his rage, he hadn't paid attention to the music, or to his own cue. Karen stretched and rolled around trying desperately to fill bars and bars of music. Finally, she sat up and smiled at her less-than-charming prince, who returned her look with a scowl. As the curtain fell on Act II, Rudolf announced that he would not dance the final act because he had hurt his foot. No one was terribly surprised, as steel lighting stands aren't very forgiving, but his understudies had long since left the theatre to catch a late movie. After extending the intermission for 45 interminable minutes, Rudolf grudgingly agreed to perform the last act.

Rudolf was tired of the National Ballet and tired of Canada. He had guest appearances booked all over the world for the next five years, and he wanted Karen to come with him. Becoming a full-time guest artist meant leaving the company. "I can't, Rudolf," Karen said. Her heart belonged to Canada. She couldn't leave the National Ballet permanently, even if it meant a successful international career. Even for love. As strange as it seemed, the National Ballet of Canada was Karen's second family. She had grown up within its walls, and she wouldn't have achieved her dream of becoming a ballerina if it hadn't been for Betty and Celia. "You can't be happy schlepping about the provinces," Rudolf countered. Maybe it was guilt and obligation, maybe it was a sort of patriotism, but Karen Kain would not leave Canada.

A ballet star could tour the world and make five times the salary of a principal dancer at the National Ballet. She could have artistic freedom through the power of her status, and dance any role she wanted, almost anytime. But Karen didn't relish the idea of living out of her suitcase for the rest of her life. She wanted stability that she didn't yet have, flying constantly back and forth from Europe to Canada to the United States.

Chapter 9
To Fall and Rise

By the late 1970s, Karen Kain was, by Canadian standards, a superstar. Her life was tracked by the media, just like any Hollywood celebrity. Plagued by perfectionism since she was young, Karen never felt she could meet the expectations she perceived from the public. The pressure was immense. For Karen, every performance had to be perfect. Everyone was watching. Her unhappiness began to come out in her interviews, which in a way, had been foreshadowing all along. "I enjoy working, just working," Karen is quoted as saying as early as 1971. "Killing myself until I'm nearly sick."

And she did love working. Every rehearsal was a performance for her. She danced with full intention and energy every time. While others would "mark" the movements at the back of the studio, Karen danced her heart out in the centre. After a day of rehearsals was through, she would often stay behind, going over and over the difficult movements until they were perfect. Karen was always emotional. It was part of what made her such a wonderfully expressive dancer — through dance she could express everything from pure joy to abject terror. She was a sensitive person, known for tears of frustration in rehearsals and classes.

Celia left the National Ballet in 1974. The company's founder and artistic director for 23 years departed abruptly, amid rumours and in-fighting with the board of directors. After Celia left, the company entered a very tumultuous time. Celia's co-director David Haber took over, but was promptly fired a few months later. Celia returned briefly, but was gone for good by 1976. After a makeshift artistic leadership comprised of the company's resident choreographers and rehearsal directors, the company's status in the ballet world was threatened. As difficult as Celia was to work with, she had done amazing things with what had begun as an amateurish, untrained band of dancers. Under her leadership, the National Ballet of Canada climbed the ranks of the international ballet scene and came out as one of the leading companies in the world, alongside the famous Russian Bolshoi Ballet and Britain's Royal Ballet. But now, as the company faltered without strong leadership, things were getting desperate.

Alexander Grant, a former dancer and director of Britain's Royal Ballet, came on as artistic director in July of

1976. Optimism swept through the company, as Grant was known as a man of great humanity and talent. Grant treated the dancers as adults — at the time, a novel concept — asking for their artistic contributions to roles and ballets. In Celia's era, and in some of today's ballet companies, the men and women are referred to as "boys" and "girls." Such patronizing treatment was thought to keep the dancers in line, requiring of them the same unquestioning obedience as children. Grant would have none of it. He asked dancers for their opinions on artistic approaches and input on the choreography. Unfortunately, his soft-handed approach would be his downfall; he simply wasn't a strong enough leader to run a ballet company.

Desperate for everyone to like him, Grant wasn't able to make the difficult decisions an artistic director needs to make. While he brought some famous British ballets to the National Ballet, he wasn't pushing the dancers or the company forward. He taught them the roles that he had made famous, but didn't acquire many new ballets. The public and the critics felt that the National Ballet was drifting, and the dancers did, too. After four years of flimsy leadership, Grant began coming late to his own rehearsals. Once there, he'd get the dancers reviewing what they worked on last time, and promptly fall asleep. The dancers, including Karen, were getting angry. Karen had committed to the National Ballet because she believed the company was capable of great things, and she wanted to be part of its growth. But this was stagnation.

Karen made a special appointment to speak with the president of the National's board. Even though she felt like an outsider with all of her touring, she thought her position might have just enough weight to make a difference. She told the president that the dancers weren't being pushed enough, and that the public was noticing their mediocre performances. As she spoke, his gaze seemed to blur her out. "The National is sliding downhill," she said. The president nodded, and thanked her for expressing her concerns. A week later, Alexander Grant's contract was extended for another three years.

A drastic change was required in Karen's personal life as well. Karen and Frank took up where they had left off after Karen's relationship with Marcel. However, Frank couldn't shake the feeling that Karen was simply looking for something stable and comfortable to hang onto. In the beginning, he didn't mind. He was just happy to have her back in his life. Eventually, Karen's touring schedule became impossible, and the pressures all around her felt like they were closing in. Meanwhile, Frank felt as though Karen had begun to hang onto him for dear life. His career was going well; he'd been invited to guest perform with a few companies, but his injuries held him back. An injured knee and weak back would plague Frank for most of his career, seriously limiting his potential. He was comfortable at the National Ballet, and knew instinctively that he would never go too far. Still, he felt like a crutch for Karen's insecurity — an instinct that would prove correct.

To Fall and Rise

In 1979, Karen hit the proverbial wall. She was unable to continue at the same frenzied pace. All of her vacation time from the National Ballet had been filled working for other choreographers and other companies. After the season with Roland Petit at the Paris Opera, she told him, "That's it. I'm quitting. There's no joy for me in this anymore." He put his arm around her and suggested she take a few months off. She spent the summer with friends and family, but as soon as rehearsals began for the National Ballet, she was there. Her misery continued. Plus, her partnership with Frank began to crumble as well.

It happened quite suddenly, after one of many trips to France. Without warning, she became demanding, yet distant. "Look at me here," she would say. "Look at me with love in your eyes, with some fire." She was anxious and short-tempered. It was as though she was more important than Frank. She had moved on, and forward, without him. She no longer listened to Frank's ideas and they weren't working together the way they used to. It wasn't intuitive and natural. In fact, it was quite the opposite — it was cold. This is how other dancers worked, but not them. They had always been different.

Frank held her close in a lengthened arabesque, waiting to feel the intangible signal, a slight shift of weight, a nuance in her spine. Nothing. It was as though she was made of stone. His stomach dropped.

Karen's frustration with the National Ballet had reached its peak. She could have been dancing every night in exciting ballets with thrilling choreographers if she had taken Rudolf and Roland up on their offers. She wondered why she even bothered to stay. In 1982, Karen missed the National's spring season because she was working with Roland in France. A reporter in Toronto asked Alexander Grant why he had allowed Karen to miss the season. "Perhaps Karen is a little more special," Grant said. "She has more leverage. What can we do?" Alexander had essentially told the press that Karen was a prima donna. That she was using the National Ballet as a home base, but had no real commitment to the company whatsoever. Karen was incensed. How could Alexander say such a thing, when he knew the sacrifices she had made to stay with the company? By suggesting she had broken her contract with the National Ballet, he was threatening her public image.

Karen's mind was racing. What could she do? She had gone to the board president to no avail. Clearly, Alexander was not on her side. She had no choice. When a reporter from *The Globe and Mail* asked if she wanted to comment on Grant's allegations, she jumped at the chance. Going on public record was the only way to get heard, and she was willing to do it. She spoke frankly about Alexander and how she felt the company was falling apart. She explained how she was made to feel like a second-class citizen at the National Ballet for her guest engagements when she had never broken a single contractual agreement. "I've got to stand up for myself," Karen said. "It's clear that the National won't stand up for me."

The board had no choice but to react. They announced that Alexander Grant would be asked to leave a year before his contact expired. Karen's bravery had paid off, but her relationship with Grant was permanently altered.

By 1979, every day became a struggle for Karen. Her limbs felt impossibly heavy, and moving through daily class was exhausting. She wanted nothing more than to sleep, and on days when she had a spare hour between class and rehearsal, she did. She would burst into tears inexplicably on the subway, in class, in rehearsal. It was humiliating. On top of it all, she felt guilty for not staying at the studio and working through a difficult exercise from class, or getting a head start on the day's rehearsal. Performances became terrifying. Unable to control her anxiety, Karen would have full-scale panic attacks before performances.

Standing backstage before one such performance, she could hear the audience rustling in their seats, and the rumble of conversation. She quickly went over her movements in her head, certain that she would forget something. She went through a simple preparation and took off for a practice pirouette, but her balance was off and she teetered to the side. Mortified, she tried again. This time, she made it around and landed perfectly. It didn't matter. She thought it was just a fluke — she was terrible and always had been terrible. Every good performance she had ever given was a coincidence. She had no real talent; she had fooled everyone.

Somehow she got through that performance, and many others. However, as more time passed, things really began to fall apart. Celia Franca, retired by this point, attended one of her performances. She came up afterward and quietly cautioned Karen about burning out. Her reviews weren't complimentary. What was happening to Karen Kain?

Karen was heartily criticized for her apparent lack of commitment to the National Ballet of Canada (even though she had already exceeded her contractual agreement by 10 performances, with half the season left to go). Karen took these things very personally, and felt as though she was letting both the company and Roland Petit down. Perhaps she was. Without being fully committed to either institution, both had to make do without her, and deal with the repercussions of her fatigue.

Karen was exhausted during class and rehearsals. She was getting the dances confused, having to remember so many at one time. She was irritable and short-tempered. In any given month, Karen would perform up to 10 different full-length ballets, each more than two hours of dance. Unfortunately, it was her problem, not the National Ballet of Canada's. Other dancers wanted a chance at the limelight. They were waiting for the opportunity to take a starring role, but the public wanted to see Karen, and only Karen. The dancers were hurt and angry, and their feelings were directed at her.

No one could see that Karen was trying to please everybody. She wanted to make the National Ballet of Canada happy, and bring them up to the level of international acclaim she felt the company deserved. She wanted to work with Roland because she was perfect in his eyes. After the humiliation at the dancers' meeting, working for him was a nice break. There, she felt like a princess, and was treated like one.

One night after a performance of *Giselle* in Toronto, Betty Oliphant came backstage to congratulate Karen. Betty found her sitting all alone, staring off into the middle distance. "Karen, you were wonderful," Betty exclaimed.

Karen looked at her, confused and miserable. "It was terrible," she said, her voice flat. Betty's eyes narrowed as she continued to look at Karen.

"How is everything?" Betty asked.

Karen shook her head with what looked like a huge effort. "I want to quit," she said, beginning to cry.

Betty, as usual, pulled no punches. "Karen," she said sternly, "you are seriously depressed and you need to get help." Within days, Betty had arranged for Karen to see a psychiatrist.

Karen worked steadily in therapy, seeing her doctor almost every week. There she was able to identify her tendencies to please everyone at the expense of herself, her perfectionism, and her workaholism. But epiphanies such as these do not happen without casualties.

Chapter 10
Endings and Beginnings

Since the mid-1970s, Frank Augustyn had lived in the shadow of Karen's growing international career. As she flew all around the world, guest performing with this company and that company, Frank was often left home in Toronto, performing with the National Ballet. Their partnership was celebrated into the late 1970s, but only when Karen happened to be home, and the two of them happened to be dancing.

Frank sat in the lobby of the National Ballet's studios, sipping tea in the middle of the afternoon. A young female journalist sat beside him, leaning in, and eagerly asking him what it was like to be Karen Kain's partner. Frank looked at her. Her eyes were shining, and maybe, he thought, she had wanted to be a ballet dancer at one time. He sipped his tea thoughtfully, recalling the number of times in the past year a journalist much like this one had asked him the same question. Too many to count, he mused, as he cleared his throat. "A good partnership is a rare and great thing," he said. "I am lucky to have found such a thing with Karen." The young journalist scribbled furiously on her pad of paper, and Frank suddenly felt guilty for giving such an empty answer.

For years, Karen and Frank had worked together, dined together, performed together, and slept together. But when Karen visited Frank in Brussels in 1981, they both knew it was over. They sat in Frank's hotel room, Karen on the bed, and Frank in an overstuffed chair. They barely had to speak about it. They had been together a total of seven years, and Karen had left him twice. After both episodes, Frank had taken her back. But this time, something was different. Karen sobbed, but Frank remained dry-eyed. He knew that he had been holding onto something that was no longer there. For a while afterward, he hoped vaguely that she would come back. She didn't.

That night, Frank had a strange brush with the supernatural. He was staying in the Hotel Metropole in Brussels, an old hotel with creaky, hardwood floors. He collapsed into bed and pulled the blankets around him, hoping for comfort. He heard someone walking along the hallway, the floor creaking with every step. The steps moved closer to his room. There was a click on the ceramic tile inside his door, and the sound of steps continued along the floor of his room. The steps moved to the left side of his bed, and then to the right. A neon sign outside the hotel lit the room enough for Frank to see that no one there. He sat up. Once again, the steps creaked toward the foot of his bed. "Please go away," he said. "I'm really tired." Frank lay back down uneasily. After a moment, the steps creaked away from his bed, clicked across the tile and made their way back down the hallway. It was as though the ghost of Frank and Karen's relationship had visited him, and had gone away for good this time.

After their relationship ended, Karen and Frank danced together only on a few occasions. Karen was still searching for that holy grail of the perfect performance, pushing him to go further with every role. But Frank was tired. They had danced the same dances for almost 10 years now. Karen pushed him and pushed him, often dragging rehearsals late into the evening. Frank had simply had enough. "Karen, I'm finished," he said one evening as rehearsal crept toward 8:00. "I'm hungry and I'm tired."

She pleaded with him to dance the section one more time, which in Karen's vocabulary meant 10 more times. Frank stood back and scrutinized her. There were bags under Karen's eyes and her face was pale. Her hair was a mess and her clothing seemed to hang off her body. He shook his head sadly, picked up his things, and walked out of the studio.

After that, it seemed Frank's desire to dance his former roles came to an end. He no longer wanted to dance *Swan Lake* or *Giselle*. He wanted something new, and the conclusion of his partnership with Karen was the catalyst. Frank began dancing contemporary ballets by young choreographers, and guest performing in Belgium and London. Eventually, he left dancing altogether, becoming the artistic director of the Theatre Ballet of Canada, which later became the Ottawa Ballet. Doomed from the beginning due to unrealistic expectations from the board of directors, and shifts in Canada Council funding, Frank was forced to retire five years later. He married and had children; he filled his life with love, and work always came second to his family.

Karen, too, would eventually find true love. It happened in 1981 at a rehearsal just before a gala performance celebrating the National's 30th anniversary. To this day, Karen doesn't remember meeting Ross Petty. Ross was a Canadian actor, working and living in New York City. A year later, he was back in Toronto headlining a production of the musical *Sweeny Todd*. He, of course, remembered Karen, and asked a mutual friend to invite her to opening night. She planned to refuse; after all, she had no idea who this person was.

She dialled Ross's phone number, prepared to decline the invitation on his answering machine. But he picked up. As soon as she heard his rich, deep baritone voice, she found herself changing her mind. They met for dinner after the show, and this time, Karen would not forget the dark-haired handsome man with the soulful brown eyes. They had a wonderful evening, and she left the following day to perform in Italy.

When Karen returned from the Italian ballet festival one week later, *Sweeny Todd* had ended its run, and she figured that Ross had returned to New York. She opened the door to her apartment, dropped her keys and her bags, and pressed the button on her answering machine. A deep voice poured out saying, "I'm still in town, and for only one reason." Karen felt her heart jump as she dove for the phone. They went out to dinner that night, and Karen was smitten.

Four months later, Karen and Ross sat in the kitchen of his apartment. It was October and they'd had a lovely day walking the streets of New York, holding hands. The two had just come back from a seafood dinner at a local Italian restaurant. Karen's heart was pounding and she felt light-headed. She couldn't place where this idea had come from, even though it felt so right. "Will you marry me?" she asked. Her eyes went impossibly wide and she clamped her mouth shut. Ross looked stunned. Then, his face softened and he smiled.

"I'll never let you eat the mussels there again!" he teased. They looked at each other. The idea had come as a surprise to them both.

Their courtship was fast, and most of it was spent planning their wedding. As a national celebrity, Karen's life had been under the media's microscope for more than a decade. Deciding to marry someone virtually unheard of was upsetting for the public. "What's-his-name better treat her good," was journalist John Fraser's response, and Karen's family wasn't much warmer. It seemed her family — and indeed all of Canada — assumed that she'd literally marry prince charming. But marry they did, in May 1983.

Karen and Ross assumed they would split their time between Toronto during the National Ballet's season, and New York, where Ross's acting career had taken off. However, the realities proved to be more complicated than they'd imagined. The couple endured what amounted to an unsatisfying long-distance relationship for several months.

Yet another stolen weekend with her husband had come to an end, and Karen sat on the couch feeling miserable. Her bags waited by the door for the taxi that would arrive in 20 minutes. The night before, Karen and Ross had compared schedules, sitting over dinner with their two day-planners spread open as though they were business partners, not husband and wife. Karen opened a new production at the National Ballet soon, and Ross didn't finish his run of an off-Broadway show for another six weeks. They wouldn't see each other for at least one month. They had shrugged it off the night before, but now, with only 15 minutes left together, it all felt too real.

They sat in silence, Ross with his arm around Karen. "I'm moving to Toronto," Ross said after a long moment. Karen was thrilled: she could keep her position at the National Ballet, and Ross had gained enough experience acting in New York; he'd get tons of work in Toronto. Or so she thought. As with most things, the reality of a situation proves far more complicated than the dream. Ross had braved the incredibly competitive theatrical communities of New York, Paris, and London, but nothing would prepare him for his return to Toronto. Circumstances were changing quickly for the couple, and there were more surprises to come.

In early 1988, when she was almost 37 years of age, Karen went for a routine physical. About an hour later, Karen burst through the front door of her Cabbagetown home. Ross was reading a book in the living room. He looked over to see his wife, grinning like a madwoman, her hair tousled. "We're having a baby," she declared.

With a baby on the way, Karen's performance season would end early — to the public, this would seem most conspicuous. She was scheduled to appear in France in the summer and New York in autumn. All of these engagements would have to be cancelled, and fast. In the several days that followed, reporters began showing up outside her door and waiting for her after class. They wanted to know why she was cancelling her international shows. The National Ballet of Canada was about to make its season casting announcement, and Karen knew there would be speculation about her absence in the season. While she was only two months pregnant, Karen knew she had to make a public announcement. Uncomfortable at the idea, and feeling it somewhat premature, she arranged a press conference for the following week.

A few weeks after the announcement, Karen woke up nauseated. Ross was away in Vancouver producing a television show, and she had slept in late. She went downstairs to the kitchen to make some herbal tea, plugged in the kettle, and leaned against the counter. Suddenly, a terrible pain sliced through her lower abdomen. She started sweating as she doubled over. She tried to remain calm and breathe deeply, but she didn't know what to do. Another bolt of pain shot through her body, and she fell to her hands and knees. A pool of blood was forming on the stark white linoleum. As she began to sob, the kettle started to scream.

More than three months into her pregnancy, Karen miscarried. The next day, she got on a plane headed to Vancouver. Ross was waiting at the airport, his face red and streaked from crying. They held each other for a long time. Five days later, Karen was back in Toronto; she had promised Erik Bruhn, her friend and mentor, that she would host his first dance competition. Karen's friend Glen Tetley met her backstage and held her close. He whispered in her ear that everything would be all right. Then, the curtain opened and, once again, Karen Kain went onstage.

After the miscarriage, Karen threw herself into her work. Dancing had always been her solace in times of struggle; it was how she dealt with loss in the past, and it was how she would deal with it now. Although Karen's compulsion to please everyone had led her to depression, Karen would still struggle with this tendency into the 1980s. She bounced back from her breakdown with incredible stamina, receiving a stellar review in the *New York Times*. She was no longer a ballerina past her prime, giving lacklustre performances and spreading herself too thin. She was Karen Kain, prima ballerina. And she was back.

The Canadian media debated whether she would stay with the National Ballet of Canada, or leave to work internationally. Reporters bantered back and forth about what the National would have to offer her to stay. Roland wanted her for six months of the year at the Ballet de Marseille. She also had opportunities with Baryshnikov at the American Ballet Theatre.

After Alexander Grant's public humiliation and subsequent absence, the National Ballet was poised for either great success, or another failure. The board was under pressure to do the right thing, and fortunately it did. Erik Bruhn came to the National Ballet of Canada in 1983 as the new artistic director. A brilliant dancer, choreographer, and natural leader, Erik was the best thing that ever could have happened to the National Ballet of Canada.

Erik began his career in his native Denmark with the Royal Danish Ballet. A star by 20 years of age, Erick was one of the few men to become truly famous in the world of ballet. He danced through the 1950s and 1960s with the American Ballet Theatre, partnering some of the best ballerinas in the world. Rudolf Nureyev and Mikhail Baryshnikov, both flamboyant, media-savvy dancers, generally eclipsed Erik's fame. Erik was known for his subtlety and commitment to the art of ballet. Like Karen, he was a workaholic, suffering from ulcers for most of his life as a result of his intense, high-strung personality.

Erik brought the National Ballet of Canada the strong direction it needed. He pushed the dancers to become the best performers they could be, firing those who were lazy or unwilling to go the distance. He brought new ballets and revivified the classics. He was the reason Karen stayed on with the National Ballet, and why she never regretted her decision. So, it came as both a shock and a tragedy when, at the age of 57, he was diagnosed with advanced lung cancer. Doctors discovered the tumour in March, and by April, he was dead. Lying on his deathbed in late March 1986, Erick wrote a letter to the dancers of the National Ballet. In it he said, "Let's go on from here, spirits up, with confidence, belief, and mutual respect for each other — not only to go on, but to go on inspiring each other."

In November 1988, the National Ballet hosted a gala celebrating Karen's 20th anniversary with the company. A huge, splashy affair at the Royal York Hotel, the event included a program of dances selected by Karen, a dinner, and a "roast," which offered an opportunity for the guest of honour to be teased by colleagues and loved ones alike. Ross had been asked to speak, and he worked for weeks getting his speech just right. However, the evening went differently than he expected. What was to be a roast became a heartfelt toast, with old partners, choreographers, and journalists bestowing warm anecdote after warm anecdote.

Nervous and unable to think clearly, Ross walked up to the podium and cleared his throat. As he began to speak, he felt separated from his body. He heard himself saying what sounded like bitter jokes about being in Karen's shadow. On autopilot, he found himself uttering sardonic references to old boyfriends. It was the speech he had rehearsed, but now it all seemed to come out wrong. Karen sat at the table, all eyes on her, with a false smile plastered on her lips. Her parents sat stiffly by her side, bristling with anger.

Moving to Toronto had been incredibly challenging for Ross. Despite working in New York and London, his résumé counted for virtually nothing in Toronto. It was a smaller centre, and there simply wasn't that much work to go around. Theatrical runs were shorter, and actors' salaries much smaller. The media kept close tabs on Ross, the husband of Canada's Sweetheart, making the pressure for success almost unbearable. All the attention was centred on his marriage to Karen; no one cared whether he could act.

Karen listened to the speech, and finally understood Ross's frustrations. She saw how difficult it had been for him to stop his career and move to Toronto for her. She understood what it must have felt like to be seen as "Karen Kain's husband," rather than an individual. Ross's dissatisfaction was all too evident, and his anger was coming through right now, at her anniversary gala.

The applause was hollow as Ross stumbled down from the stage, his face pale. Karen got up, made her way to the podium and began to speak. She thanked Ross for his speech and for tolerating her over the past five years. She cleared her throat and tried to smooth things over by telling a few funny anecdotes from her years with the company, but the damage had been done. Her perfect marriage was obviously nowhere near as perfect as she had thought.

Ross entered therapy soon after, hoping to resolve his feelings of jealousy and resentment. Karen joined him, and the two of them worked hard to repair the problems that had undermined their marriage.

Erik Bruhn, also driven by his work, could have empathized with Karen's dilemma. His commitment to dance and choreography came at the expense of personal relationships. In fact, he and Rudolf Nureyev had been lovers for years before Erik broke it off so he could pursue his work uninterrupted. Much earlier, when Karen's partnership with Frank was unravelling, Erik had advised Karen to "dance her own dance." But now, in the wake of depression and burnout, was she really willing to let her marriage get crushed under the weight of her illustrious career?

A dancer's career rarely lasts past the age of 30. Even now, with advances in medical knowledge, such as physiotherapy and alternative medicine, it is unusual to see a dancer over the age of 40. All good things must come to an end, and somehow Karen had kept going. She had loved and lost. She had danced all over the world. She had been a star, dining with the rich and famous, from Hollywood actors to the Prince of Wales. But fame has its costs, and Karen had paid handsomely in relationships and with her own health.

Karen had missed out on the contemplative side of life. Now, as her marriage hung in the balance, she had to make a choice.

For Karen, dance had always been the most important thing in life. Her passion and ambition had driven her throughout her career, often at the expense of relationships, and certainly at the expense of a normal life. Her obsession led to depression and exhaustion, but also to new heights of artistry in ballet. Karen was a true artist, a person whose life is just as devoted to her purpose as that of any religious leader. However, there comes a time in life where ambition and experience transform into wisdom — when the urgency of the early days mellows into confidence. Karen Kain, the artist, could now choose her path through the world of dance. She was no longer 22, tossed around like a leaf in the wind. This was her life, her dance, and she would direct her next steps.

Epilogue
Karen Kain's Legacy

aren Kain's life was more complex than those of the princesses and fairy queens she portrayed in dance. She battled depression and the exhausting life of a touring artist, watched closely by the media, but plagued by loneliness. She sacrificed several relationships for her love of dancing and her fierce commitment to her career. Karen saw many of the world's most beloved dancers retire or die. Tragic losses to the dance world included Erik Bruhn and her long-time partner and mentor, Rudolf Nureyev, who died in 1993, after a long struggle with illness.

Karen continued to perform after that dramatic anniversary dinner in 1988 — for eight more years, in fact. She stayed on as a full-time company member at the National Ballet of

Canada, creating some wonderful new works that pioneered a place for maturing dancers in the world of ballet. Combining the richness of maturity and the depth of her experience, Karen gave some of her most celebrated performances during this time.

In a teary press conference in 1996, Karen Kain bid adieu to the stage after a prolific career spanning almost 30 years. She stayed on as artistic associate with the National Ballet of Canada, and was named the company's new artistic director in June 2005. In 1976, she became an Officer of Canada, and accepted the even higher honour of becoming a Companion of the Order in 1991. In 1996, Karen Kain became the first Canadian to receive the Cartier Lifetime Achievement Award. She holds honorary degrees from York, Trent, McMaster, Brock, and the universities of British Columbia and Toronto. Karen is also the founding president of the Dancers' Transition Resource Centre, assisting dancers with career options after retirement from the stage. She and her husband, Ross Petty, live a quiet life at their farmhouse just north of Toronto.

Karen Kain in *The Actress* (1996)

Further Reading

Augustyn, Frank and Barbara Sears. *Dancing from the Heart: A Memoir*. Toronto: McClelland and Stewart, 2000.

Darling, Christopher and John Fraser. *Kain & Augustyn*. Toronto: Jonathan-James Books, 1977.

Franca, Celia and Ken Bell. *The National Ballet of Canada*. Toronto: University of Toronto, 1978.

Jackson, Jenny. "The making of Karen Kain," *Edmonton Journal*, Edmonton, Alberta: September 10, 1997. Pg. C6.

Kain, Karen with Stephen Godfrey and Penelope Reed Doob. *Movement Never Lies: An Autobiography*. Toronto: McClelland and Stewart, 1994.

Neufeld, James. *Power to Rise: The Story of the National Ballet of Canada*. Toronto: University of Toronto, 1996.

Acknowledgements

This book could never have been written without the support of some very important people. First, thanks to Stephen Hutchings, Kara Turner, and Jill Foran from Altitude for including dance among such a celebrated collection of incredible tales. Extra special thanks to Karen herself for her inspiration, and her invaluable help on this project. Thanks also to Jennifer Nault for suggesting the idea in the first place; it's amazing what a well-timed e-mail can do for a person's career. Sincere and deep thanks to my dear friends and colleagues at St. Joseph Media in Calgary for all their support: Jennifer Annable for her flexibility and humour, Dulcy Bentler for keeping my priorities straight, and, of course, Andrew "D" Mah, for being one of my dearest friends of all time. Deep thanks and love to my parents Allan and Charlotte, my sisters, Angela and Kim, and my dear friend Alison, for their unending support and love, no matter what. And thank you to all the characters in my own dance history: Anne, Christine, Keith, Darcy, Damon, Michele, Helen, and Natalie.

Photo Credits

Cover: The National Ballet of Canada Archives; The National Ballet of Canada Archives: pages 8, 44, 76 (photographer Ken Ball), 117; Chad Shier: page 121.

About the Author

Melanie Jones is a freelance author and editor. She worked as Editor of WHERE Magazine for three years, and was a freelance dance writer for several years before that. She performed as a contemporary dancer for seven years, and an actor for five. She holds a Masters degree in Dance from York University in Toronto and a Bachelor's degree in Dance from the University of Calgary. She is also a marathon runner, and will be competing in the Boston Marathon in 2006. She will also be contributing to Altitude Publishing's new series, Late-Breaking Amazing Stories.

Amazing Author
Question and Answer

What was your inspiration for writing about Karen Kain?

When I was a young girl, my uncle gave me a biography of Karen Kain filled with photographs. Karen Kain and I both have long dark hair and dark eyes, and I wanted to be just like her. I took ballet classes as a child, but lost interest. Then, in university, I rediscovered dance and performed for more than seven years. While in graduate school in Toronto, Karen was invited to speak at one of our seminars. Sitting there, across from my childhood heroine, I could barely say a word!

What surprised you most while you were researching Karen Kain's life?

I was surprised by how hard Karen Kain was on herself. She is one of the most well-known Canadian dance artists of our time and yet she never thought she was good enough.

What do you most admire about Karen Kain?

I admire her single-minded focus and dedication. She gave up a lot that most of us take for granted. The life she chose (or did it choose her?) was not easy; it took years and years of sacrifice to achieve what she did.

What escapade do you most identify with?

I identified most with the performances. I used to perform a lot and I love the combination of fear and exhilaration. There is nothing quite like being on stage, and I got to relive that through this book.

What part of the writing process did you enjoy most?

I loved writing the dancing sections. As a former dancer myself, I find it so enjoyable to translate movement into words, so a reader can really feel what it's like to balance and jump and turn and soar.

AMAZING STORIES
ALSO AVAILABLE!

AMAZING STORIES™

ROBERTA BONDAR

The Exceptional Achievements of
Canada's First Woman Astronaut

BIOGRAPHY
by Joan Dixon

ROBERTA BONDAR
The Exceptional Achievements of Canada's First Woman Astronaut

"The feeling in space flight is like hanging by your heels...with all the blood rushing to your head. ...You feel as though you are at the top of a roller coaster when your stomach feels like it is going to lift off."
Dr. Roberta Bondar

From the age of eight, Roberta Bondar knew she wanted to be an astronaut. In January 1992 she made Canadian history when she became the first Canadian woman, and first neurologist, to go into space on board Discovery. The story of her journey to become a leading astronaut is a fascinating tale of dedication, commitment, and sheer guts.

 True stories. Truly Canadian.

ISBN 1-55153-799-0

AMAZING STORIES

ALSO AVAILABLE!

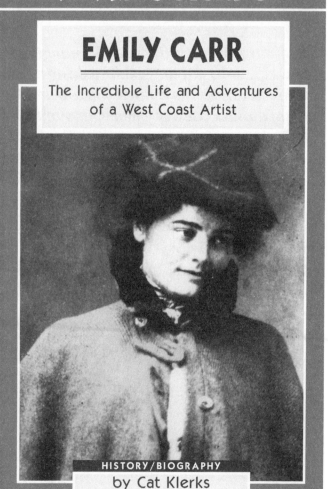

AMAZING STORIES™

EMILY CARR

The Incredible Life and Adventures
of a West Coast Artist

HISTORY/BIOGRAPHY
by Cat Klerks

EMILY CARR
The Incredible Life and Adventures
of a West Coast Artist

*"On a sketching trip with her friend Edythe
Hembroff, Emily made the other woman swear
not to peek while she hastily slipped into her
nightie. This was odd considering how cheerfully
Emily would defy social convention in many
other ways. The woman who loved to shock
others was quite easily shocked herself."*

This is the story of a rebellious girl from BC who
travelled the world in pursuit of her calling, only
to find her true inspiration in the Canadian
landscape she'd left behind. Despite numerous
setbacks, she persevered. Today, Emily Carr is a
Canadian icon. Her story is a testament to indi-
viduality and an inspiration to all.

 True stories. Truly Canadian.

ISBN 1-55153-996-9

ISBN	Title	ISBN	Title
1-55153-959-4	A War Bride's Story	1-55153-951-9	Ontario Murders
1-55153-794-X	Calgary Flames	1-55153-790-7	Ottawa Senators
1-55153-947-0	Canada's Rumrunners	1-55153-960-8	Ottawa Titans
1-55153-966-7	Canadian Spies	1-55153-945-4	Pierre Elliot Trudeau
1-55153-795-8	D-Day	1-55153-981-0	Rattenbury
1-55153-972-1	David Thompson	1-55153-991-8	Rebel Women
1-55153-982-9	Dinosaur Hunters	1-55153-995-0	Rescue Dogs
1-55153-970-5	Early Voyageurs	1-55153-985-3	Riding on the Wild Side
1-55153-798-2	Edmonton Oilers	1-55153-974-8	Risk Takers and Innovators
1-55153-968-3	Edwin Alonzo Boyd	1-55153-956-X	Robert Service
1-55153-996-9	Emily Carr	1-55153-799-0	Roberta Bondar
1-55153-961-6	Étienne Brûlé	1-55153-997-7	Sam Steele
1-55153-791-5	Extraordinary Accounts	1-55153-954-3	Snowmobile Adventures
	of Native Life on	1-55153-971-3	Stolen Horses
	the West Coast	1-55153-952-7	Strange Events
1-55153-993-4	Ghost Town Stories	1-55153-783-4	Strange Events and More
1-55153-992-6	Ghost Town Stories II	1-55153-986-1	Tales from the West Coast
1-55153-984-5	Ghost Town Stories III	1-55153-978-0	The Avro Arrow Story
1-55153-973-X	Great Canadian	1-55153-943-8	The Black Donnellys
	Love Stories	1-55153-942-X	The Halifax Explosion
1-55153-777-X	Great Cat Stories	1-55153-994-2	The Heart of a Horse
1-55153-946-2	Great Dog Stories	1-55153-944-6	The Life of a Loyalist
1-55153-773-7	Great Military Leaders	1-55153-787-7	The Mad Trapper
1-55153-785-0	Grey Owl	1-55153-789-3	The Mounties
1-55153-958-6	Hudson's Bay Company	1-55153-948-9	The War of 1812 Against
	Adventures		the States
1-55153-969-1	Klondike Joe Boyle	1-55153-788-5	Toronto Maple Leafs
1-55153-980-2	Legendary Show Jumpers	1-55153-976-4	Trailblazing
1-55153-775-3	Lucy Maud Montgomery		Sports Heroes
1-55153-967-5	Marie Anne Lagimodière	1-55153-977-2	Unsung Heroes of the
1-55153-964-0	Marilyn Bell		Royal Canadian Air Force
1-55153-999-3	Mary Schäffer	1-55153-792-3	Vancouver Canucks
1-55153-953-5	Moe Norman	1-55153-989-6	Vancouver's
1-55153-965-9	Native Chiefs and		Old-Time Scoundrels
	Famous Métis	1-55153-990-X	West Coast Adventures
1-55153-962-4	Niagara Daredevils	1-55153-987-X	Wilderness Tales
1-55153-793-1	Norman Bethune	1-55153-873-3	Women Explorers

These titles are available wherever you buy books. If you have trouble finding the book you want, call the Altitude order desk at **1-800-957-6888**, e-mail your request to: **orderdesk@altitudepublishing.com** or visit our Web site **at www.amazingstories.ca**

New **AMAZING STORIES** titles are published every month.